THE UNLIKELY EXECUTIVE

FROM DOPE AND DESPAIR, TO LEADERSHIP AND LEGACY

JEREMIAH WHEELER

Copyright © 2025 by Jeremiah Wheeler
First Paperback and Hardback Edition

All rights reserved. No part of this publication may be reproduced, distributed, or transmitted in any form or by any means, including photocopying, recording, or other electronic or mechanical methods, without the prior written permission of the publisher, except in the case of brief quotations embodied in critical reviews and certain other noncommercial uses permitted by copyright law. For permission requests, write to the publisher, addressed "Attention: Permissions Coordinator," at the address below.

Some names, businesses, places, events, locales, incidents, and identifying details inside this book have been changed to protect the privacy of individuals.

Published by Freiling Agency, LLC.

P.O. Box 1264
Warrenton, VA 20188

www.FreilingAgency.com

PB ISBN: 978-1-963701-68-5
HB ISBN: 978-1-963701-69-2
E-book ISBN: 978-1-963701-70-8

DEDICATION

Dedicated to Chesney, my strongest advocate and biggest fan. Your love and grace gave me the courage to become the man I was meant to be.

CONTENTS

1	My Childhood	1
2	My Parents Divorce	9
3	My Life as a Teenager	17
4	Trouble With Dad	25
5	Motorcycles Become My Life	35
6	My Wife	45
7	My Career	55
8	The Repo Business	63
9	My Sister	75
10	A Time of Grief	87
11	My Nephews	93
12	My Experience in Rehab	99
13	I Find the Other Side	117
14	Moving Forward	123
In Memory of Robert Morris		137

> "We were young… but everything we saw, heard, or did was filtered through what we believed God expected from us."

1

MY CHILDHOOD

My family used to go to church three times every Sunday.

We did this for years. I'm not sure exactly how many—I was too young to keep track. Long enough, I suppose, that those whirlwind days would be forever impressed upon my memory.

We'd wake up with the sunrise—early enough to hear the birds chirping before we could even see them. Mom would cobble together some kind of breakfast while we played with each other, and maybe with Dad, in our tiny living room. Or, if it wasn't too hot, outside in the front yard. Eventually she'd call us in, we'd sit down, Dad prayed, we'd eat, then we'd dress up in firmly-pressed shirts and blouses, all tucked tight into modest pants and skirts pulled up past our belly-buttons.

(Only years later did I realize, and appreciate, just how much time and effort mom must have spent ironing those clothes the night before. And she did this for other families, too—there's no telling how many pieces she pressed over the years.)

Around 8:30am, we'd pile into my dad's S-10 pick-up truck—my parents, my big sister, my little brother and me. We'd squeeze all onto one row (there was no backseat), which made it almost impossible for my dad to shift gears. I remember everyone being mostly drenched in sweat by the time we closed the doors, but nobody complained about the heat. Then I'd watch out the window for the seven-and-a-half minutes it took to drive to the First Pentecostal of Jesus Christ Church in Woodville, Mississippi.

It was at this church—built from the ground up (literally and figuratively) by my father, his brother Steve, his first cousin Jimmy, and a few future congregants—that I first learned about God. I remember watching my father preach boldly from the pulpit about whatever had been on his mind that week. And even more vividly, I remember the confident "Amens" (sometimes whispered, sometimes shouted) and never-ending nods of approval from the people sitting around us who, for various (and sometimes ill-advised) reasons, considered my father a suitable spiritual leader for this fledgling, but very serious, community of "born again" believers.

The church was Pentecostal, through and through. And in true 1980s, Southern Gospel style. The preaching was fiery, the singing was loud, the repentance seemed real. We raised our hands, moved, even danced. We prophesied about things we didn't understand. We laid hands on the sick and prayed, some of us, with full expectation of complete and total physical healing.

The spirit was at work, as they say. Woodville was a small town, home to no more than 2,000 souls. Our church was attended by about 100 of them. But that congregation on those Sunday mornings was our world and a place where, as Dad used to say, "God is at work."

This wasn't unlike many other churches and religious communities thriving in that rural, even wilderness, corner of Mississippi during the 1980s. Historians say the Deep South has long been the country's heart of innovation in religious expression—a place where God was being lost and found over and over again, each time with more fervor (so everyone thought) than the last. For whatever reason, Pentecostalism struck a chord at this particular time. It was like a revival. And my young parents found themselves swept up into the middle of it.

After these lively morning services, known to run anywhere from one to three hours long, my father would gather us all back into his hot pick-up truck and drive to another, even smaller church about 15 miles west of Woodville where he'd preach the same sermon again to another lively crowd at First Pentecostal Church of Centerville. It was like the morning on repeat. We'd sing the same songs, pray the same prayers, and listen to dad preach the same thing all over again. Then we'd turn around and drive back to Woodville for evening service, where we'd listen to Dad preach yet again—three times in one, long day.

That was normal life for us. Lots of preaching and teaching. The same thing, week after week. We were trying to please the God who came down to us through Jesus, but most immediately through my dad's mind as he read and studied and preached. We tried our best to "live right." This meant no drinking, and certainly no drugs. It meant lots of Bible reading and talking with each other about things of God. We'd have people over to pray. We'd visit sick members of our church and lay our hands on them as we asked the Holy Spirit for healing. We dressed plainly, but enough that it was conspicuous and signaled to the world just how serious we were about what we believed.

We were young. Us kids were in early elementary school, and my parents weren't yet 35 years old. But

My Childhood

ours was a life lived on purpose. Everything we saw, heard, or did was measured up and tested against our understanding of what God's Word had to say. What didn't pass muster was quickly trimmed off.

But in the end, I suppose it was all too much.

Before I was 10 years old, my dad quit pastoring. I was too young, at the time, to read between the lines. But I imagine our local friends and family had questions—those of them, at least, who knew the young, enthusiastic pastor better than to hang on every word he said. He was leaving two churches, after all. And to my knowledge, he didn't have another job offer in hand. But I imagine most people liked him and his fiery sermons well-enough to believe anything other than that God had some bigger and better plan for our family.

We moved what little we had two hours northeast to Jackson. I remember riding in the passenger seat of the car, watching billboards fly by, air conditioner on full blast. The trunk was full of our things, and I understood that, somehow, the rest of our stuff was being driven up later in a pick-up truck by a member of our congregation (though I don't remember there being much stuff to move into our new house, or maybe nothing else at all aside from whatever was already stuffed into the trunk and between the two front seats).

Our new home was a small place somewhere on the east side of Jackson, technically in a small town called Pearl. It was comfortable enough, but the city vibes were new for us, and I think also for my parents. In fact, everything felt new and unfamiliar at that time. Maybe that's why my dad's new self-declared "job" as an independent "gospel evangelist" didn't strike anyone as strange enough to speak up and say something about it. I don't know whether he was getting paid any regular salary, but at least for a time, he took this new role seriously.

Evangelists are roving pastors, so to speak. They preach the Word wherever the Spirit blows—too passionate about the Gospel to be confined to any one place or church. For our family, this meant we traveled all over the state, always by car, and watched Dad preach to different Pentecostal congregations most weeks—sometimes during morning service, sometimes during the evening. Some churches even rolled out the red carpet and hosted a weeknight "revival" service, always preceded by a big, warm dinner for all five of us at some church member's house. We even ventured as far as Louisiana and Alabama, following the Spirit's call, and the calls of any pastor who had a few hundred extra dollars to spend and a congregation hungry for more preaching than he wanted to give.

My Childhood

I'm not sure whether this afforded my family any kind of regular income. I suppose it's a blessing that I was too young to care about the kind of clothes I wore or the kinds of cars we drove. We regularly stayed with families that attended the various churches where my dad preached, and they always seemed more than happy to provide our food and lodging. Eventually, my dad bought a travel trailer and he would stay on the road preaching. We'd join him when we could, but he often traveled alone.

Now, as an adult with children of my own, it's hard to imagine this lifestyle "working" for very long—especially with three by-then pre-teenaged kids in tow.

And indeed, it wasn't three years before we moved back to familiar southwest Mississippi, this time to a town called Natchez, and again without much of a plan for how to pay the bills.

But this move was easier to understand. I'd been born in Natchez some 12 years earlier. So Natchez was, literally, where my life began. But in another, more meaningful way, it was this return to Natchez, 12 years later, that marked the beginning of Jeremiah Wheeler's story.

> "Dad was gone. Mom was free. My brother, sister, and I were along for the ride."

2

MY PARENTS DIVORCE

Technically, Natchez is the 28th largest city in the state of Mississippi, and Mississippi is the 36th largest state in the country.

I suppose this makes Natchez a small town, though it didn't feel that way to my teenage eyes in 1993. Even coming from Jackson.

But to be fair, there isn't much outside of Natchez in any direction. So it's someplace, even if nothing special. To the west, across the muddy Mississippi River (which, at times, literally engulfs parts of the town), lies a few hundred square miles of wet Louisiana bottomland—perfectly flat and very, very wet. The alluvial soil in this area is exceptionally productive for cotton farming, and, aside from a few large wildlife refuges dotting the region, cotton farms still cover almost the entire region.

To the east of Natchez is Mississippi wilderness. One could, and can still, walk in a straight line for almost a full day through the forests of Adams County without seeing much, though the landscape is always dotted with patchwork clearings left behind by loggers. The bear, deer, foxes, possums and beavers are plenty. Alligators, too. Forest-related activity accounts for a good portion of the county's economic output today, and probably more than that when my family showed up in 1993. And I can remember several plants manufacturing various goods and materials and employing a good chunk of the population. Those jobs paid well at the time, but NAFTA put a quick end to most of those outfits.

But my father wasn't in the logging or the manufacturing business. And in fact, around 1993 is when he decided he wasn't going to be in any business—not even religion. His church days were over. I'm not sure if he quit so much as he just stopped trying. Remember, he'd been an independent "evangelist," and so had no real ties to any particular community. By the time we got to Natchez, I think his gigs had simply disappeared, slowly but surely. I don't remember him ever working much in Natchez, aside from some odds-and-ends construction jobs. He was home a lot

And to my memory, as soon as we showed up in Natchez is when he and my mom started fighting.

My Parents Divorce

Our house in Natchez was small—even smaller than our humble place in Jackson. It was a mobile home, and I don't know whether we owned it or rented. It sat in a rough neighborhood called Cloverdale on the southwest edge of town, and my parents had a few friends and family members living close by. It seemed like everyone knew everyone in Natchez, and gossip traveled fast. But even this didn't keep my parents from shouting at each other, usually in front of us kids. They argued—even screamed—at each other about things I didn't, and still don't, understand. Probably, some of it had to do with money. I realized later that much of it had to do with alcohol, and sometimes drugs. Either way, wheels were falling off, and whatever semblance or appearances of Christian piety my parents had put on over the past decade were quickly swept into the dustbins of a history that immediately began to seem false.

I learned only later that my parents had been typical "hippies" in their teenage and early-adult years, before my siblings and I were born. They partied hard in south Mississippi—lots of drugs, lots of alcohol. That was all new to the area at the time. Southwest Mississippi had been, and still is, rural and quiet. But the 1960s brought a lot of new experiences to the area, and my parents were as caught up in it as one might expect any pair of bored teenagers to be. My mom had been married twice before my her and my dad.

So, it was a bit of a shock to those around them when they got married and decided to become ministers. I heard it all happened pretty fast. Maybe too fast. I wonder how many of their friends and family members were skeptical of their "conversion" and their new plans to devote their lives to ministry. Could anyone have imagined my father preaching three times every Sunday? A traveling "evangelist?" But the fact is, somewhere along the way, they "found Jesus." And I suppose, from the perspective of their families, it didn't matter what exactly that entailed so long as it meant staying sober and settling down.

And for all intents and purposes, that's what they set out to do.

Anyways, no matter how it happened, Mom and Dad's outlook on life changed fast, and they dove headlong into the Pentecostal church movement that had begun sweeping across the South, pews filled with thousands of erstwhile hippies just like them. And for about 10 years, that life sustained them and the three kids they would have along the way.

But eventually, back in Natchez, the alcohol and drugs showed up again. And looking back, I'm not really sure they ever disappeared entirely. I hadn't been around drugs much as a young kid, so I didn't notice, at first, when my dad was drinking or high. But something was off between him and mom once we moved back to Natchez—this was obvious to me, and I imagine to everyone else in town.

Then one day, as I sat outside on our broken front step listening to my parents fight, my dad packed up and left. He moved around for a few months before settling in south Louisiana with his sister, who he, along with everyone else in her community, knew had what he wanted.

Mom and dad got divorced. It was quick. It all happened within a year of moving to Natchez. Dad had made his decision, and my mom immediately got eager to break free from the Pentecostal mores that had, from the start, always been stricter than she liked. No more long skirts. No more plain face and straight hair. She completely changed her look, in fact. I remember this vividly. She started going to bars, meeting up with friends, and having a good time. She dated different men, often leaving my siblings and me to fend for ourselves—even late into the night.

But we didn't mind this. I felt like she cared about us, and for us. We always had a roof over our head and enough stuff to do. We went to school (though we didn't study much). She'd even give us money when we asked for it, and if she had it. If she didn't have it, she'd ask whoever she was dating at the time. We got to see her sisters and her old friends, none of whom had followed her to the church, and who, I imagine, were all happy to have her around again.

Dad was gone. Mom was free.

My brother, sister, and I were along for the ride.

> "I had two different identities—and I didn't realize how dangerous it was to live in both."

3

MY LIFE AS A TEENAGER

It wasn't long before mom more-or-less settled down with an older guy in Natchez who owned a feed-and-farm store just outside of town. We'd ride our bicycles all over the place, and we'd often stop by the store to try and get her to ask him to give us chips and soda. He obliged, but never without making us work off every single penny. We usually found his propositions agreeable enough and spent 15 minutes here-and-there picking up around the store and around the cluttered lot outside.

One day he offered me a steady job sweeping the floors and stocking the shelves after school. A 13-year-old should be busy.

It was my decision, ultimately, though my mom all but insisted I say yes. But fact is, $3 an hour was a pretty enticing offer for a teenager who, alongside his mom, had just started to discover how much fun one could have with a little freedom and some cash in hand. I hardly needed her opinion. I took the job, and eventually did a lot more than just sweep and stock. We bagged and stacked 50-lb sacks of feed. We baled hay in the summertime out in the fields. We loaded trailers until the blisters got too bad to keep going. My "bosses" (my mom's boyfriend and his son Chad) were pretty straight-laced, and we did everything the right way. I learned that hard work pays—a lesson I took to heart and, to this day, I've never, never forgotten.

But he was a hard-ass, through and through. He yelled a lot. He'd tell us we weren't working hard enough. That would make me mad and I'd think about quitting, but the spending money was too important to me. I suppose the experience was pretty good for me, all said and done.

I got paid every other Friday (or sooner, if I worked hard enough and could talk some extra spending money out of him). $30, $60, sometimes $90. It was a lot of money for a 13 year-old (and a lot of hours). And it wasn't long before I decided exactly how I wanted to spend it.

Almost a decade earlier, my dad bought a little Suzuki 50 motorcycle for my brother and me. We'd ride it around the yard, sometimes down the street. We literally rode the tires off it more than once. It was tons of fun.

It just so happened that my mom's boyfriend's son Chad (one of my "bosses" at the store) raced off-road motorcycles almost obsessively—street bikes, motocross, and everything in-between. He had bikes, his cousins had bikes. Even his girlfriend rode a dirt bike. These were some of the only young adults I knew, and watching them race around that motocross track down behind the hayfield got me hooked.

I can remember laying in my bed one night thumbing through motorcycle magazines, adding up my rate and hours to see what I might be able to afford. Motorcycles weren't cheap. I got into BMX. My friends, my brother, and I would ride our bikes four-and-a-half miles from my house to the BMX track, spend a full day racing, jumping, whatever, then ride all the way home again. Same bike the whole time. We rode them ragged (like I said, I was hooked).

My mom's boyfriend had a 1989 Honda CR125 that he'd rebuilt from the ground up. It was in excellent shape. Sometimes, if I worked hard enough, he'd let me ride it and race it. Like I said, the work was hard, and I didn't always like it, but the thrill was worth it to me. The harsh words and lack of any kind of affirmation was a small price to pay for going fast and jumping high on the back of that Honda.

Eventually, I lived to ride. I don't know if this was healthy for a teenage boy, but my mom was too busy to care. And besides, I'd been exceptionally responsible for a kid my age. I worked every day after school. I saved my money. I looked out for my siblings and, except for when biking, was pretty cautious about things, in general. I didn't want to get in trouble. At 14 years old I was already smoking weed and hanging out with a rough crowd. I failed the 9th grade twice and by 17 dropped out of school. My mom didn't care or understand the importance of education. She let my older sister drop out too

But over the months and years, I suppose this caught up with me. I kept working and saving and racing , but I eventually developed two very different circles of friends—even two separate identities. On one hand, I was the responsible kid who worked every day. Other kids like me noticed, and we'd hang out to ride or fish or hunt (never to study). On very rare occasions, I even went to church with them a few times. On the other hand, I was into BMX, and a lot of kids on those dangerous race tracks were running away from tough family situations. I didn't think I was like them, at the time, but I was around them a lot, and I joined in on their shenanigans often enough to look cool enough.

Those shenanigans weren't always harmless, though. The older I got, the more drugs I saw. And the more drugs I saw, the more willing I became to take a hit, now and then. It was never too much—like I said, I was cautious by nature. I worried about getting in trouble more than I worried about not spoiling the fun.

But the fun wasn't hard to spoil, I learned. These friends didn't care if I joined in, but they liked having me around, which made me feel good. I got pretty comfortable with them. Eventually, smoking pot in the woods by the BMX trails and at friends' houses became buying weed from local dealers. And eventually that became trips to New Orleans with friends dead-set on maximizing every minute and every dollar spent during our long nights there.

For a 16 year-old kid from Natchez willing to try almost anything, New Orleans was quite a place. Even without the religious mores weighing me down since mom decided that moving on from dad meant moving on from church, the expectations on energetic teenagers in the Deep South were heavy (even if not always truly expected). Life in Natchez could feel stifling. But New Orleans was a big hole where all of that disappeared. The city was full of possibility. It celebrated individuality and excess. It was fun without second-guessing—no looking-back.

And in New Orleans, the drugs were easy to get.

So we started going down after work on the weekends, even leaving after dark. It was a two-and-a-half hour drive, so this meant a pretty late start. We'd smoke pot on the way down. We'd drop LSD at the State Palace Theater when we got there. We'd party all night until the sun came up and then, sometimes, head back toward Natchez the next morning.

We did this a lot. Looking back, it's a wonder we survived those nights, and those long drives. We were young—15, 16, maybe 17. We were drunk and high. We were clueless about the dangers that lurked around every corner as we fumbled around New Orleans late at night, or just how much trouble we'd be in if we were pulled over somewhere along the way. I'm not sure we understood that selling dime bags to finance our escapades could have landed us in jail.

But survive, and even thrive, we did. Somehow. And for better or worse, I never had to learn anything the hard way.

Yet.

> "This wasn't the dad I needed. I wish he'd known that."

4

TROUBLE WITH DAD

I'm not sure what other kids thought of me back then.

I partied hard. Most of my friends and classmates knew that. But I was always worried. I didn't want to get caught. I didn't want to get hurt, and I didn't want my friends to get hurt, even though I wouldn't let them know that.

I can remember one particularly late night in New Orleans, after some concert, corralling my friends into the car after my brother Nate pissed off some guy outside a rave in the Palace Theater. Things got tense, and it was apparently funny to everyone but me. The guy was big and about 20 years older than us. I was sober enough to see that this wasn't going to end well.

It was me who suggested leaving, me who got the car, me who drove us home that night three hours back to Natchez. To this day, I wonder what might have happened to Nate and the rest of us, if I hadn't let my better judgment (and anxieties) take over that night.

The truth is, I found myself in this situation a lot—not always totally sober, but enough to know my left from my right, and to know that I cared too much about my own safety to let things turn dangerous.

But if I was so worried, why did I put myself in these situations? Because deep down, I knew they were always dangerous, no matter how worried I was, deep down, about getting in trouble. I wasn't even 18—why did I keep doing something that made me so uncomfortable?

As I look back on those blurry New Orleans nights, bass pounding and strobe lights flashing, I see now that I was searching for something I didn't know I was missing. It was something specific, but I couldn't name it. It was something I'd know when I found it, but didn't know where to find it.

The fact is, it was never the allure of the parties or the drugs that fueled my late-night and all-night escapes to New Orleans. I wasn't chasing a high. I wasn't running away from anything at home in Natchez, where I had all the freedom I wanted. But in those moments of recklessness, I mistook the pounding of my heart for the pulse of liberation, the rush of adrenaline for the thrill of belonging. But now, with the clarity of hindsight, I see that I was simply trying to fill a void that no amount of noise or distraction could ever mend.

I was looking for acceptance. I couldn't have spelled this out at the time, but hanging around these guys—as nervous as they made me—felt good. They (mostly) accepted me for who I was. They pushed me, but they respected me, and they cared enough about me to call me every time they were headed to New Orleans (or wherever) to hang out. That meant a lot more to me than I let on, and I hung a big part of my hat on how they thought about me. Like so many teenagers, we shared the common bond of family dysfunction. Nothing good was going on at home. Even those of us whose families seemed happy enough were more than ready to "screw the man."

Looking back, I can see the whispers of conscience that I ignored, the nagging doubts that I brushed aside in my quest for acceptance. Deep down, I knew that this wasn't who I was meant to be. I knew that I was betraying a piece of myself with every puff, ever drink, and every laugh forced through gritted teeth. But I was too young, and too insecure, to face the truth staring back at me from the depths of my own reflection. I shouldn't have had to figure this out on my own. I was too young. I was left to my own devices too much, and didn't have the kind of guiding influence a kid needs from authorities who love him.

But the hard truth lurked there nonetheless. The truth was that I missed my dad.

It had been about three years since dad left. It all happened pretty fast. We moved back to Natchez, my dad mostly out-of-work. His passion for the ministry had completely faded, and was maybe never real—only God knows. But out of money and out of work proved too much for his constitution, and his fights with my mom were more than enough reason, I suppose, for him to bail out.

I hadn't seen him much over the years. The divorce was fast, like I said—there was no scheduled visitation or court-ordered anything, really. He left us with mom, and she sent us down to see him every few months. I'm not even sure this was part of any agreement—it's just something mom decided we ought to do every so often. Most of the time, he stayed with his sister in South Louisiana and smoked a lot of pot. For work, he pulled live crawfish from traps while working at a crawfish farm in Crowley, Louisiana.

I can remember driving up to his house. He'd walk out, smile, seemed happy enough to see us. He'd make us food, make sure we were comfortable. We'd chat about life in Natchez. He'd ask about mom. He smoked a lot. Every once in a while, his sister would stop by to say hi. She was always nice—to us, at least.

But as I got older (probably 16), dad didn't sit right with me. I remember once sitting in his living room. He had all sorts of questions about our lives and what we were into. The topic of drugs came up.

"Ya'll do drugs?" he asked. I didn't know how to answer. He seemed like he just wanted to know how we'd answer, and wasn't too concerned whether it was a yes or a no.

"Sometimes," I said sheepishly.

"What do you do?"

"Uhh, I mean. Smoke pot." Dad nodded wistfully.

"You do any hard stuff? Any LSD?"

I shrugged my shoulders. He stared me down.

"You stay away from that hard stuff," he said. "It's not good."

"Yeah, I know."

"Here, I'll be right back." Dad got up and walked into his room, then came back out with a bag of weed. He showed us how he rolled his joints, gave us each one—my sister, my brother, and me—and we smoked together inside. He didn't say much, and we didn't know what to say. It didn't feel right, but it was my dad.

That's how it started to go with him most visits. He smoked a lot of pot, and he decided he'd bond with us that way—I think, maybe, he didn't know how else to do that. Sometimes he'd show us some other stuff—ketamine, speed, snorting Oxycontin. He'd teach us how to use them "properly," to maximize the high. We'd do this for a few days, maybe see a few more of his friends, and then we'd go back home to mom. She didn't care what kind of drugs we did. She didn't care at all.

This happened several times over the years. And, looking back, I realize I didn't think much of it at the time. Getting high with your dad isn't a good thing to do, but he was my dad. Hanging out with him was a rare privilege, and getting high with dad was even cool. The fact is, nothing about my community in Natchez and beyond made this kind of behavior seem wrong. Sure, a deep-down part of me had some doubts about him. I think I was maybe a little disappointed. But a teenage kid is told where to go, what to do, and it's easier to try to have fun along the way than to start questioning everything. My life was the only life I knew. I got good at lying to myself about the doubts and convincing myself that there was nothing wrong with what I was doing—drinking, smoking, raising hell in New Orleans all through the night. And I tried to love my dad, and my mom. I didn't want life to be harder than it had to be.

But this wasn't the dad I needed. I wish he'd known that.

Looking back, it's hard for me to understand his evolution from pastor to drug addict. What was all that preaching about? All that hard work pastoring congregations across two towns? All the evangelism across three states? Was it something we should forget ever happened because it clearly didn't matter now? Is God really *there,* or is it all just games of imagination—a phase some people go through?

I didn't hold onto the past because it was gone and maybe full of false ideals. I didn't know what the future was supposed to look like, or what kind of man it was possible for me to become. I didn't like my dad as much as I thought I did, at the time, but I didn't know where else to turn—most of my influences were teenagers or men my mom was dating and who I'd rather not be around.

I was lost. A big part of me was empty. And I didn't even know it.

That is, until I got a job working for Robert Morris.

> "The same emptiness inside that I tried to fill with long, buzzed nights in New Orleans was being filled with motorcycles—and increasingly, with Robert."

5

MOTORCYCLES BECOME MY LIFE

Back home in Natchez, motorcycles had become my life. What had begun a few years earlier as a weekend BMX hobby—a way to meet new friends—had become the most important part of my teenage identity. In Mississippi at the time, a kid didn't need a license to ride a "dirt bike," so I wasted no time.

I was first introduced to motorcycles a few years earlier by one of my supervisors at the feed-and-farm store—he'd ride laps around a track he carved out around the edge of the property where we bailed hay, complete with jumps and whoops and everything in-between. It was exhilarating to watch.

So as soon as I saved up enough, I bought an old dirt bike from someone just outside Natchez—a well-used red Honda. That thing flew. I started by riding it around the track behind the hay field I'd spun around so many times before. I can still remember every bump, every turn. I must have circled that thing 5,000 times.

Eventually, I moved onto bigger and better venues. I raced cross-country enduro races all over the southeast and also raced motocross tracks from Texas to Alabama. The whole scene was intoxicating for a 16 year-old teenage boy whose mom didn't care what he did (as long as he "didn't do nothin' stupid"). We raced, we rode loud-and-proud through town sometimes, and got into trouble more than once.

We also came dangerously close to seriously injuring ourselves way too often. It's a wonder I, or any of my buddies, didn't die going 50 miles per hour, virtually alone and a good 5 miles from the nearest hospital.

I remember one muddy afternoon jumping a large double behind the bike shop and overshooting the landing.I landed so hard that both of my hands came off the bars and I slammed my chest onto the bars and crashed. I had broken my left wrist from the impact. With my body in shock and me feeling no pain, I figured I could still ride. So that's what I did. No point in ending a good day if I could still stay on the bike. After a few more laps, I realized something was wrong and ended up in the hospital and later, a cast. As I got better at riding, the local races caught my attention. Natchez was home to to a big motorcycle shop. There were a few good motocross tracks within a couple hour drive from Natchez and we tried to go as much as possible. The local tracks would host races and events every so often—real, official things with sponsors and an audience, depending on who showed up. Every so often, some 20 year-old from out of town would drive up with a shiny rig and brand new bike, donned head-to-toe in a matching outfit featuring the name of some store or even a manufacturer plastered in big letters across his chest. He'd win and hang around afterward for pictures and to talk up his sponsors. Then he'd ride his bike up into his trailer behind a new F-150 and hop into the passenger seat. His dad or his brother (or whoever) would start the engine and drive off to some other event, all looking to my teenage boy eyes like the coolest man in the entire world.

That's who I wanted to be.

I practiced riding almost every single day. The gas wasn't cheap and my grades took a backseat. But in a roundabout way, the obsession was good for me. It's good for teenage boys to keep busy. This was a serious hobby—some intentional way for me to spend my time that got me caring about things like gas prices, saving money, and working extra hours in order to buy some new tires or replace some part. I had a goal. I wanted to be the best motocross rider in Natchez. I wanted to be the best motocross rider in the world.

Eventually, I started spending a lot of my free time at House of Cycles—a motorcycle shop off Highway 61 on the outskirts of town. At the time, it was the biggest bike shop in Natchez, and the only serious dirt bike dealer. I'd walk the rows of bikes I couldn't afford, learning everything I could. I dreamed of riding them. I talked to the dealers and mechanics and sometimes to the middle-aged guys who came in to buy some Kawasaki or other, probably for their son who had no idea just how lucky they'd be to get one. I don't know why I hung around there so much. Maybe I'd meet someone who'd get me in somewhere, or buy me a bike. Or someone who'd seen me race, maybe, and who'd take note of my interest and help me out. I had all sorts of hopeful scenarios cooked up.

Sure, all of this was extremely unlikely. I was just a kid. But like I said—I was obsessed.

And believe it or not, something did happen. Or, rather, someone. His name was Robert Morris.

I'd met Robert before. He owned the dealership with his dad and they sponsored all sorts of events around the area. I saw him at the store all the time, but he was always busy—usually cutting up with some customer or parts manufacturer. I spent every minute I could at that store and would sweep around the mechanics in the back, asking them a million questions. I would ask Robert to let me work there and he would laugh and say "you aren't quite old enough yet, but come back and see me when you turn 16". I did exactly that and he offered me the job. I started work the next day.

In some ways, those first few months at House of Cycles were the most thrilling of my entire life. I was living my teenage dream in real-time and learning my craft from a man who, I'd soon discover, was just about the best person who could have walked into my life at the time.

Robert was a Mississippi native. Born and raised in Red Lick just north of Natchez, he and his dad purchased House of Cycles in the 90s and they both worked there just about every day. It was really Robert who moved things along. He was a people person with a knack for business. He knew motorcycles inside and out and owned several himself. Apparently he first started riding at age five. But his real skill, and he knew it, was building relationships. In fact, it's hardly fair to say he thought about his customers as "customers," at all. Robert just loved people, and he'd smile with genuine joy anytime someone walked in the front doors. He trusted them, and they returned the favor.

I hung around Robert's dad Jake, too. He was a country guy and still lived, I think, up in Red Lick. But Robert was only about 15 years older than me, and we connected on a deeper level. We were friends—not just colleagues. Robert was a mentor to me from day one. He took an interest in my life. He answered my questions. He encouraged me to dive even deeper into my passion for motorcycles, and helped me understand how this hobby might turn into a business—even a decent living—for me in the not-too-distant future.

Robert and his dad had their fingers in anything motorcycle-related that happened within three to four hours of Natchez—races, events, shows. They'd drag me along to all of this. On our long rides there and back, Robert would go on and on about his family, his kids, the business. He taught me about the local economy, the idiosyncrasies of the motorcycle market, how things I saw happening on TV in Jackson and in Washington affected the price of gas and people's willingness to pay for dirt bikes and such. We'd listen to the radio some, when the conversation died down, and he'd add his commentary, explaining why this or that was good or bad.

Motorcycles Become My Life

He was a devout Christian, too, and his faith infused just about every thought he ever had—even business.

He was a talker and a teacher. And because he also happened to be cool, I soaked this all up.

It wasn't long before Robert suggested that House of Cycles sponsor my riding. He'd seen me compete in a few local races, and I suppose I was good enough that it was worth his time and money (although I sometimes think he might have done this for me no matter what). I like to think it was because of my skill. But either way, this sponsorship really set me up. Suddenly, other brands started to care about me, too. Husqvarna gave me a bike at next-to-nothing, so I had two bikes at one time—one for motocross, and one for enduro.

Things were getting serious.

We raced all over Mississippi, Louisiana, and Alabama. We even made it up to Arkansas a few times, riding what was called, back then, the Southeastern Enduro Circuit. Sometimes we'd be in the truck for eight or nine hours at a time, hauling a load of bikes on a fifth-wheel behind us. That thing took hours to load up. But the rides were fun. Robert would talk, I would listen. His dad would chime in; they'd talk business, I listened to every word. The business of motorcycles became part of my passion, too, and I started to put together my future.

I said before that this obsession was good for me, intense as it was. Meeting Robert only made that truer. I was a motorcycle guy—I didn't want to be anything else. And I wanted to be like Robert. He was the right kind of person to idolize.

I often wonder if these are the kinds of thoughts and feelings I might have had about my dad, had he not ran off a few years prior. Kids need their dads—boys especially. Dad gives context to the world, and puts a teenage boy in his place. I've learned this as a father myself, and I saw it happen back in at the races with kids whose dads showed up and took an interest in what their son was doing (and in making sure he was safe). In a way, I miss what I never really had. I wasn't bitter, at the time—not on the surface, at least. But I was missing something. The same emptiness inside that I tried to fill with long, buzzed nights in New Orleans was being filled with motorcycles, and increasingly with Robert. I looked forward to our car rides almost as much as the races themselves.

Robert knew about my life. He knew I'd dropped out of high school. He knew I smoked pot and got drunk a little too often.

But Robert believed in me, and I'd do anything I could to never let him down. He told me time and time again that I could be anything I wanted and my family didn't define me.

> "I met the girl of my dreams, and I started to see the world through a new lens."

6

MY WIFE

There I was. 18 years old. Riding motorcycles all over the South, chasing thrills and learning everything I could about the motorcycle business. I had my own bikes. I had a sponsor. I worked almost every single day at the bike shop. In my teenage mind, my life was coming together. I'd ride and sell motorcycles forever. I'd be big in the business. I'd figure out how to do this all the time. I wanted to be rich.

But in one way, all of these dreams were moving a bit too fast for me. I was still a kid. I had all but failed high school, so I dropped out. There were other relationships, too, that I left by the wayside—a few too many loose ends, I think, that I wasn't tying up. But I still worked hard at the dealership and, looking back, I suppose I seemed pretty responsible to most people. My mom still didn't care too much.

Anyways, Robert was looking out for me, and knew how much I loved to ride. Being neck-deep in motorcycles was fun, and it mostly kept me out of trouble.

But looking back, I think everything happened too quickly. I was still living a double life. I worked hard during the day, but smoked pot at night—often with the same high school buddies who seemed to do nothing but smoke pot all day long. I had a job, sure. But the more I immersed myself in the motorcycle world, the less I knew about who I was outside of that. Somewhere deep down, this bothered me.

But then I met someone who changed everything.

I had just turned 19. My old supervisor at the feed-and-farm store—the first guy I ever saw race motorcycles around the state of Mississippi—was throwing a birthday party for his now-wife. They were a few years older than me, but we'd stayed close over the years (Natchez wasn't a big place, after all). They invited me.

I didn't always attend these kinds of things. Usually I had a race. If I didn't, I'd sometimes make up some reason not to go and ride bikes or smoke pot with friends, instead. But I liked this guy, and I figured they'd have free booze.

The party had gone on for about an hour. I'd been hanging out, drinking some, making small talk with the few people I knew. A lot of them were people we raced with and we all had those things in common.

I had some small glow sticks, one of which was in my mouth. Then this girl walks up and asks me if I had any extras that she could have. I gave her one and she moved on.

Never in my life, before or since, had I been so struck by someone's presence—just the fact, and sight, of them in front of me. I felt an immediate, supernatural connection. I knew, at that moment, that my life would never be the same.

She soon found out that would be true for her, too.

We talked for few a seconds, I think. Then she walked off. I was smitten. I didn't even know her name, and I was pretty sure she was a good deal older than me. But after she turned around and walked away, I spent the rest of the evening asking around about her, trying to learn everything I could. I didn't care what anyone thought I was trying to do. It turned out she was one of my friend's big sisters—24 years old, a college graduate, and a registered nurse and she had a boyfriend.

In other words, she was a very different kind of person than me. But I didn't care.

I learned her name was Chesney, and eventually I got her number. That wasn't easy. becoming friends, running into each other around town at local hangouts. I was pursuing her even though she didn't know it. One day I asked her what it would take for a guy like me to date a girl like you. In the nicest way she could she told me a girl like her wouldn't date someone like me. She explained that she had worked very hard to be successful and independent and would never date someone who had dropped out of highschool, never gotten a GED or taken an ACT and who smoked pot everyday.

That hit me, and hit me hard. Looking back, meeting her was like a big whiff of smelling salts. It woke me up and got me going like nothing else—even more than my motorcycles. Suddenly, I didn't care about who I'd wanted to be before. I dropped all that as quickly as I'd picked it up. I met the girl of my dreams, and I started to see the world through a new lens. I was totally committed to doing whatever it took to clean up and get this girl to like me.

I quit smoking pot literally that day. Cold turkey. I signed up for my GED a few days later. I passed, then signed up for and took the ACT so I could start taking classes at a local college. All of this happened within about one month's time, and, of course, I made sure Chesney was apprised of my progress every step of the way. She and her boyfriend broke up, which was perfect timing.

Anyways, I think all this started to get her worried. Here she'd told me just about everything except "No" and listed out all the reasons why a girl like her won't ever be with a guy like me—all the reasons why things wouldn't, and couldn't, work out. And here I was undoing all the things she mentioned, turning into the kind of guy she said she wanted to be with.

I think she was equal parts impressed and confused. And maybe a little terrified.

But sure enough, we started spending more time together. We'd go out to lunch and I'd buy her meal, (though she most definitely had more money than I did). We would meet up at some of the local bars in the evening where other friends were hanging out. I told her about my family, she told me about hers. I talked a lot about motorcycles—too much, probably. She talked a lot about work, her patients, the doctors she didn't like.

I had just broken my wrist around this time and was chasing her and more focused on her. What I didn't realize is this would be the end of my motorcycle career.

Looking back, this all happened fast. Maybe too fast. Just like with my motorcycles, I'd launched headlong (or, this time, head-over-heels) into a new "adventure," this time chasing the girl of my dreams—the first girl I ever seriously dated. Pursuing her became my entire identity. I was consumed with the idea of being with her for months on end. I was only a teenager, but I was willing and ready to do whatever it took to make "us" happen. If it meant giving up pot, I'd give up pot. If it meant getting a degree, I'd get a degree. What she said she wanted became my north star.

Fast-forward a few months , and Chesney and I got serious. We spent most of every day together, when we weren't at work, and we were happy. I dreamed of our life together, and we were both working hard to do things right.

Then Chesney got pregnant.

I remember the afternoon we found out. We were sitting on her front steps, and she started crying. We didn't expect this and we weren't ready for this. We were both working full-time, trying to make ends meet. I was only 20 years old—I wasn't even old enough to buy a beer. How was I supposed to have a baby? Raise a child?

My Wife

And here was Chesney, dating some broke motocross kid who all-but cornered her into giving him a chance. Now she was carrying his baby.

Don't get me wrong. We were serious. I loved her and was willing, even as a scared 20-year-old kid, to do anything to make her happy. And she saw the best parts of me and had even started to believe that, maybe, we had a future together. But the fact is, we'd only been together a few months at this point. We weren't married, and we had no idea what to do.

Needless to say, this news hit us like a Mack truck. And yet again, everything in my life changed.

At the time, I owned three motorcycles—two for racing, and a street bike for getting around town. That street bike was my main form of transportation. I drove that thing all over south Mississippi, usually way too fast. But I sold all three as soon as I could and bought a used SUV. I sold other things, too. And I took a new job at a different motorcycle dealership that offered me more money. I worked my butt off preparing for this baby—that became my new life's purpose.

The baby eventually came, and things worked out as well as they probably could have. We got married soon after and I worked even longer hours at the dealership, trying to make ends meet. My wife kept working, too, and she was paid well, though her opportunities as a nurse were a bit limited in Natchez. We'd talk in the evenings about our days, about the baby, and about what else we should be doing to make more money. Life came at us fast, and I grew up fast. I probably had more confidence than I should have, but I was committed to Chesney and our baby, and I had no doubt about that.

Life keeps going, whether you like it or not. It's up to us whether we run along with it or fight it every step of the way. Somehow, my 20 year-old self chose to buckle up and keep on going—I think it had a lot to do with just how much I loved Chesney, and her seeing all the best parts of who I was and the potential of who I might become.

> "I knew I had to get out... My reputation and integrity were more important than staying with a company that no longer valued the principles I believed in."

7

MY CAREER

Blame the baby. Blame my almost-always empty bank account. Blame my wife for (gently) kicking my butt into gear.

Whatever it was, 21-year-old Jeremiah Wheeler was ready to work. I was ready to make some money. I wanted to get rich. I'd learned a lot about business from my mentors at the bike shop (and elsewhere) over the years, and I had begun to understand that I had a knack for sales—motorcycle sales, sure, but other things, too.

So soon after my daughter was born, we decided to move to Jackson—a two-hour drive from Natchez. We bought a small home with next-to-nothing down on a first-time homebuyer program, and I started working my tail off. Back then (and still today), Jackson was much bigger than Natchez and filled with new and lucrative opportunities.

Right away, I got a job at a motorcycle dealer in town. That was a familiar atmosphere for me. I knew the products like the back of my hand, and I could usually tell within a few seconds what a customer was looking for (sometimes even better than they could).

That job was fun. Paid the bills. But within a few months, I wanted something more.

So one day I walked into the biggest Chevrolet dealership in Jackson—and in the entire state of Mississippi—and asked for a job. I was young. I didn't have any experience selling cars. But I'd had success selling motorcycles—I guess they thought that was enough. I sure did. They asked me a few more questions, and I started work the next week.

At least on paper, car deals had a higher ceiling than motorcycle deals. Some car salesmen made six-figures, which was an incredibly high salary at the time. Those figures made my head spin, and the prospect of making so much money lit a fire under me. I dove in neck-deep.

But unfortunately, it didn't take long for me to see the ugly underbelly of how these deals were structured. The primary goal was always to maximize profits, often at the expense of the customer. From the very beginning, I was trained to squeeze as much money out of each sale as possible. The strategies we used were clever, sometimes downright manipulative. We were encouraged to push customers into loans they could barely afford, without clearly explaining the long-term costs involved.

One of the most disheartening practices was how we were encouraged to handle financing. Instead of helping customers understand their options, which is how I'd done things at the motorcycle dealerships, we focused on selling them a payment they thought they could manage—not what was financially best for them. The whole shtick was about presenting a monthly payment that seemed affordable on the surface but was inflated with high interest rates and additional fees.

For example, if a customer's note could be $700 a month, we might push for $900 or even $950 and pocket the difference. We'd hide this difference from the customer, and play dumb when they asked about the fees.

This worked well—especially with customers who didn't fully understand how these notes worked. We were told to avoid getting into detailed explanations about finance charges or the true cost of the loan. That was a grey area, as far as the customer should be concerned. Instead, we focused on closing deals as quickly as possible. It felt wrong, and it felt sleazy.

Maybe I was just young and idealistic. Business is cut-throat, and consumers have responsibility to be sure they understand what they're signing. But ultimately, this high-pressure environment prioritized immediate sales over building long-term relationships with customers. I didn't like that. I'd often think back to Robert Morris at House of Cycles back in Natchez. He taught me to engage customers on a personal level—to build trust and develop a strong reputation. But in the car sales world (at this dealer, at least), repeat business and customer satisfaction were afterthoughts. We sacrificed all that for the sake of a quick profit.

It didn't take long before this approach wore me down. Like I said, I was ready to work. I was young and I'd seen how other dealerships and companies had built strong reputations and strong financial foundations. I was looking for a real career—not just a quick profit. The car dealers' relentless focus on exploiting customers made it hard for me to sleep at night. I started to see the car sales business as a machine designed to take advantage of people—not a place to build an honest career.

Eventually, my disillusionment hit a breaking point. I decided I couldn't continue working in an industry that operated this way. The ethical compromises were too great. I felt bad about what I sold.

My Career

I knew I had to get out.

So we moved back to Natchez. We'd worked hard in Jackson, but we weren't there long. We hadn't saved much money. I'd still had in mind to work in sales. I could always go back to motorcycles. But when we moved back to Natchez, Chesney and I found ourselves intrigued by another industry. Rather than rent a place, we found a foreclosed house that we could afford. All said and done, we paid $35,000 for two bedrooms and two bathrooms. The place wasn't pretty—a "fixer-upper," as they say, that didn't look like much. But my wife was game to renovate this place while we lived in it. I had some experience with home repairs. Back in high school, I had spent a few summers and weekends working for a friend's dad who was in the home improvement business. We did all sorts of jobs—painting houses, floating sheetrock, and tackling various odd construction projects, mostly on residential properties. It was hands-on work that taught me a lot about the basics of home maintenance and renovation.

Having her family nearby helped, too—they'd often watch our daughter while we tore out walls and hung up siding.

Anyways, we turned that place inside-out. We tore out all the old carpet. We refinished the hardwood floors underneath. I even crawled under the house to jack up the pier and beam house to fix some structural issues.

We brought that home back to life and sold it two years later for $80,000—a 100% profit. You might say this ignited a lifelong passion for flipping homes. We moved at least 15 times over the next 20 years, each move another step in our ongoing "live-in-and-flip-it" adventure. This became a way of life for us, and big reason for the financial success we'd achieve years later.

But I'm getting way ahead of myself. The next few years would challenge me like nothing else. At times, "success" in any area of my life seemed like something that just wasn't in my cards.

> "Leaving that business wasn't easy. But it taught me that success isn't just about money—it's about meaning."

8

THE REPO BUSINESS

In early 2006, about 3 years after moving back to Natchez and trying my hand at Edwards Jones, a new opportunity knocked on my door.

Two of my friends from Natchez—Shannon and Sterling Gay—had just started a nationwide firm and asked if I'd help them grow it. Their father had built a successful buy-here, pay-here car dealership in Natchez that had, for better or worse, evolved into a repossession business. Lots of these kinds of consumers end up defaulting on their car payments, and the dealership had bought it's own truck and started doing the repossessions itself. Outsourcing repossessions was costly—especially for this kind of dealer (where loan defaults were not uncommon). Shannon and Sterling saw an opportunity here when other banks began calling their dad's dealership to handle their own repossessions—they knew he had a truck, they trusted him, and it was easier than calling in some bigger brand.

Shannon and Sterling wanted to take this model to the next level and expand it nationwide.

I was intrigued by their vision. It was lofty, but like I said, I was young and ready for a challenge. Their plan was to build a nationwide forwarding repossession company—we'd act as a broker between lenders and the agents who operated tow trucks. The idea was to streamline the repossession process and manage communications and assignments from one central point. We took advantage of new, technology-first workflows and systems, and we could honestly promise (and deliver) efficiency and scalability to both lenders and tow truck operators. This all was extra appealing, at the time, given the rapidly-evolving financial landscape of the early 2000s.

I jumped on board, and we hit the ground running. Hard. Our headquarters was in Terry, Mississippi—about 90 minutes north of Natchez. We worked long hours almost every single day to grow the business. And we had fun—especially because all that effort began to pay off quickly. By late 2007, we had secured contracts with 18 of the top 20 auto lenders in the US and became a key player in the repossession industry. Eventually, we employed 170 people in a big call center and were recognized around the US as one of the largest and fastest-growing repossession companies in the country.

As you can imagine, our success was exhilarating. I was just some kid from south Mississippi—no college education or formal training in any of this stuff. Yet here I was, one of the first employees and now a higher-up at the forefront of a pretty dynamic industry. And we really were "pioneers," in a way. We were leveraging new technologies in some pretty strategic and original ways to manage the flow of information between lenders and repossession agents. We adopted cutting-edge technology to automatically read license plates and make the repossession process more efficient all over the country. All of this allowed us to handle an incredibly high volume of assignments with true precision and speed. Our clients always said we were reliable, and we were usually faster than anyone else. It sounds cliche, maybe, but our growth truly was fueled by a combination of hard work, innovation, and a deep understanding of the industry's needs—just the kind of things I'd learned, and never forgot, about how to build a strong business from Robert Morris almost a decade earlier. We never stopped taking pride in building and maintaining strong relationships with our clients, and this became the cornerstone of our success. We'd really figured something out.

That is, until we got bought by a private equity firm.

Less than two years after starting this business, a private equity firm got wind of our success. Looking back, I'm not surprised—we were making waves. But I was too young to predict just how quickly this might happen. The firm made Shannon and Sterling an offer they couldn't refuse. Looking back, we were lucky because this all happened just before the banking crisis hit—six more months, and this deal never would have happened, and who knows how we would have weathered that crisis without this new investment. The deal provided a sense of validation for everything we'd been working on over the prior two years. The private equity firm brought in new resources and expertise and seemed serious, at first, about expanding our reach and capabilities. They were very interested in new technology that was popping up around the country to make repossessions easier, and we were soon invested, as a company, in dozens of technology startups working to apply new innovation in the repossession industry.

But the transition to new ownership wasn't easy. Looking back, I should have expected this, but I was still young and inexperienced at the time. The private equity firm, with its MBA-educated managers and way-too-rigid structures, made some sweeping changes to how we operated right off the bat. Understandably, they wanted to maximize profits. But they did this at the expense of the relationships that had made us successful, and that I knew would be key to any kind of success we might continue to have in the future. Key employees were terminated one after the other. Workloads were doubled. Employees got mad. The company's culture began to shift in a way that, in my opinion, felt increasingly impersonal and profit-driven.

I started clashing with the new management. I was still young, but I knew that our success was built on the strong relationships we had with our clients and the trust we had earned. I wasn't stupid. The private equity firm's focus on short-term gains over long-term relationships was concerning. I voiced my concerns about all this. I argued time and again that dismantling our existing team, which we'd built so carefully, and overloading the remaining employees would hurt our relationships and make doing business too hard.

Unfortunately, my warnings went unheeded.

The tension between the old guard and the new management reached a breaking point. Shannon and Sterling, frustrated with the direction the company was taking, decided to leave. They had built the business from the ground up and couldn't stand to see it dismantled. Other key managers, most of whom were also close friends, followed suit. It was no less than a mass exodus of the very people who had made the company what it was.

I tried holding out for a little longer, hoping that things might change. The job paid well and, by this point, I felt comfortable in this industry. But by December 2010, it was clear that the company's new direction was unsustainable. I wrote a detailed letter to the company's Board of Directors, outlining the problems with the new direction and suggesting particular ways to turn things around. But my ideas were ignored—I really hadn't expected much different. The letter was my last gasp attempt to figure this out. But I knew it was time to move on. My reputation and integrity were more important than staying with a company that no longer valued the principles I believed in. That's something I learned from Robert Morris, and I took it all to heart.

So I resigned.

Leaving that business was't easy. I'd been neck-deep in the repossession industry for years by then, working closely with a tight-knit team of genuine friends. But the experience taught me invaluable lessons about business, leadership, and the importance of staying true to core values. Looking back, it was a crash course in not only how to do business, but how to build and manage value-adding relationships. I learned that success isn't just about making money—it's about creating something meaningful and lasting. At the end of the day, what truly matters are the relationships we build, the trust we earn, and the integrity we maintain.

I was sad to leave, but proud of what I'd done.

However, despite my honest work and best intentions, a darkness had begun to creep into my life during this time. Sure, things were going well at home—we had two kids, I was making more money than I'd ever dreamed, we'd successfully flipped a few more houses. However the intense stress of managing a rapidly-growing business put increasing pressures and demands on me. Juggling long hours, constant travel, and the weight of managing a rapidly growing team, I found myself increasingly overwhelmed—emotionally, mentally, and physically.

As a teenager, I used to smoke pot. I smoked other things, too. Dropped LSD in New Orleans. Drank way too much. But I stopped all that when I met Chesney a decade prior—she insisted, and I loved her enough to do anything for her. Remember, she'd only agreed to date me if I got clean. So I flushed all my weed down the toilet and became just an occasional social drinker—all under control.

But while working with Shannon and Sterling in Terry, and then later in Jackson at our bigger office, I learned about Adderall from a few colleagues.

At the time, Adderall sounded like a miracle drug. Technically, it's amphetamine—a stimulant. It's usually prescribed to people who have ADD or ADHD and need help to stay focused and live productive lives despite their disability. But if you don't have any problem focusing already (I didn't), it just makes you speed like crazy, like living life on hyper-drive.

Anyways, a few of my colleagues in Jackson had this whole convoluted gig down to a science. They'd go to a local doctor they knew was pretty willing to prescribe Adderall (unfortunately, that kind of doctor isn't hard to find). They'd complain of some made-up symptoms—things like inability to focus and struggling to keep a job and earn a paycheck because of it. Then they'd get diagnosed with ADHD and the doctor would write them a prescription. They'd take a pill every day before work, and sometimes again at lunch, and then work like animals late into the night. The whole thing seemed mostly harmless, and I could see that their productivity clearly benefited. If they were taking it, why shouldn't I?

So I went to the doctor and did the same thing. On top of the already high-stress environment at work, I was living in a corporate apartment in Jackson during the week and commuting back to Natchez—two hours away—on the weekends. This was a lot, but it allowed me to work late into the nights during the week and hide my Adderall use from my wife. Then on the weekends, despite having worked 80-something hours that week, I could be home and present with Chesney and the kids.

In my mind, this arrangement—and this pressure—justified my drug habit

Looking back, the pace of my life at the time was unsustainable. That's obvious. I was setting myself up for failure. And I wish I'd failed, actually, because I ended up becoming addicted to Adderall.

Initially, Adderall helped me work longer hours. I felt absolutely invincible. Adderall empowered me with the energy and focus I needed to tackle my growing workload. I would multitask like crazy. I consistently worked 18 hours a day for almost three straight years—sleeping just four or five hours every single night. But what started as a seemingly practical solution quickly spiraled into dependency. I began taking Adderall in higher doses, sometimes up to 120 milligrams a day, which far exceeds prescribed limits.

The consequences were severe. I tried to hide it, but I don't think I did a good job at that. The constant stimulation began wreaking havoc on my body and mind. I became increasingly irritable and anxious. When I found a few hours to relax, I'd start drinking alcohol—a lot of alcohol—to slow down and counteract the stimulant effect. Eventually, the prescribed doses that used to work wonders for my productivity became insufficient to get me through the days, so I started taking more. And when I ran out of prescriptions, I'd buy it from others.

Though I was far from admitting this to myself, I was completely entangled in a web of drug addiction. My relentless pursuit of professional success at any cost began to cost me the things I held most dear.

"She saw the generational curses she didn't want me passing down to our children—and she had the courage to say it."

9

MY SISTER

The next few years of my life weren't like the prior years. I quit my job in Jackson after that company went south. I consulted for a while with colleagues in the repossession business. I helped stand up a new company in the space—name it, designed the logo, set up all their software and systems. But that wasn't full-time, so I took a few odd jobs around Natchez. I painted a buddy's porch. I cut grass. I cleaned up around old houses. I spent time with my wife and kids, but got pretty worried about money after a while. Eventually, a friend set me up with an oil field company. I was hired as a "Measurement While Drilling" Engineer apprentice. I traveled a bunch—south Louisiana, north Mississippi, even up to Pennsylvania. The days were long and I'd work sometimes up to three weeks on-site before I had a chance to come home. It wasn't ideal, and it allowed me to keep hiding my Adderall habit. But it paid the bills.

I sometimes hear people call these kinds of years "transition years" or "between jobs." I suppose that's true, but what people don't talk about are all the unknowns. It's not a "transition" if you don't know what's next. And I didn't know what was next.

Then two big things happened in the same month.

First, I got the best job offer of my life. It was with a data company in the repossession industry in Fort Worth, Texas. I'd struck a deal with the owner to pay my room and board during the week, because I didn't want to move my family out of Natchez. I did a lot of commuting, and being away from home so often meant I could keep up my Adderall habit (though I wouldn't have admitted that at the time). I still work for that company to this day.

Second, my sister was diagnosed with stage-four cancer. She was only 31 years old.

This news hit me harder than anything I'd ever experienced before, and in ways I never would have anticipated. My sister was only 18 months older than me. As kids, and even more so as teens, we were extremely close. For as long as I could remember, she was always there. She's in the background, and often in the foreground, of all my childhood memories. We played outside together before and after church as toddlers. We rode bikes for hours around Natchez as teenagers, looking for things to do to pass the time. In high school, she was always there when we partied or went to New Orleans or spent time hanging out at friends' houses doing teenager things. She knew who I was, deep down, and I always trusted her. We had done life together.

So getting this news, and learning on day one that her treatment was probably hopeless, was devastating.

But what made it even harder was that, since I'd got married, my relationship with her—and with the rest of my family—had soured. This wasn't anyone's fault, though it happened probably because of me. The simple fact is, meeting my wife changed how I thought about myself and who I could be. Chesney believed in me. She wouldn't let me settle for anything less than the best man I could be. She wanted me to be successful at home and at work, and that meant leaving all my negative influences behind.

Unfortunately, my family had been a negative influence in some pretty serious ways. They hadn't met their own Chesney, and being around them too often meant being around alcohol, drugs, and a generally toxic lifestyle.

So when we got married, I started to pull back. My wife had shown me how my family dynamic wasn't healthy—not for me, and not for anyone. As a teenager, getting high with my parents was something I did, but it wasn't normal. Chesney helped me see this. Helping my mom pay the bills and buy the groceries while she had the money and wasn't working was something I'd got used to, but it really shouldn't have been that way. I also bought my brother and sister cigarettes and food, while they sat at home not working. Chesney pointed that out to me. It took meeting my wife and her spending time with my family and seeing how toxic they were to me and my development. , to wake me up to this hard reality. And I really had no choice but to put some distance between me and them, all with good intentions.

So I did. And this made them mad.

Looking back, I don't think I made the wrong choice. I was in a tough spot. My wife was right—I'd never reach my potential as a person so long as I let them and the alcohol and the drugs hold me back and drag me down. We were a close family, but, probably because they were raised the same way I was, they influenced me in ways that wouldn't have allowed me to break out of the cycle of drugs and alcohol that had already started to lock me down even before I was old enough to drink.

This all speaks to the kind of person my wife was, and still is. I don't imagine it was easy to encourage me to start pulling back from my family. She saw the generational curses she did not want me passing down to our children. Imagine telling someone to stop spending so much time with their mom and siblings. Right up until I met my wife, my family had been close. Very close. But she knew I was capable of more, and if we were ever going to have a successful family, I needed to break some cycles. And she was right. When I was around them, I got anxious and things always felt chaotic. That was no way to live.

But when I started to acknowledge this, my mom, sister, and brother were understandably upset. We grew apart, and our relationship became almost non-existent. Of course, around this time I started to work hard up in Jackson, and I wasn't around as much anyways. I sometimes wonder if this is what happens to most families when kids grow up and leave home and get married—to some degree, at least. I think it does. But the difference, maybe, is that I'd made it clear to my family that I couldn't be around the drugs and alcohol and the chaos. If they were going to make these choices, I'd walk the other way. I said that out loud. This wasn't always easy to do, but I didn't have any regrets.

That is, until one day as I sat by my sister at MD Anderson Cancer Center in Houston. Suddenly, I started to feel guilty about being so distant—about not being around and missing so much of the past few years. In that moment, I resolved to spend as much time with her as I could. I'd often drive down late at night from my job in Fort Worth—a good four hours away, without traffic—to be by her side during chemo the next day.

My sister and I did grow closer during this time. Those memories are precious to me. But the simple fact is, there wasn't much time. Eventually the doctors told us there was nothing more they could do. They suggested hospice. We chose to take her home, to my house in Natchez, where my wife became her full-time caretaker. We converted my youngest daughter's bedroom into a hospice room, complete with a hospital bed. For more than three months, we cared for her there as she slowly left us. My wife changed her, bathed her, and gave her medication. I tried to be home as often as I could, even while working in a city 400 miles away.

But it was hard to be home. I didn't like seeing my sister waste away. She weighed probably 130 pounds when she was diagnosed and only 85 pounds when she died. It was hard to watch. And on top of that, my mom and bother refused to acknowledge what was happening. She was in denial, and this made things difficult for everyone. She even used some of the money donated by my sister's friends toward her medical care for a new pair of boots—something she said she "deserved." But she hung around, not willing to believe that this was hard on other people, too.

Eventually, it got to be too much. My sister passed away on January 15, 2012, and I just couldn't take it. Part of me knew this was happening—me not truly dealing with how I felt. My wife knew it, too. But I didn't know what to do. I started to question all the decisions I'd made surrounding my family—pulling away from them when I got married to focus on work, my own wife and kids, and staying clean. Sure, they would have made it hard to do that. Being around my family meant being around alcohol and drugs. But the truth is, I'd been using drugs of my own. I'd been all but addicted to Adderall while working in Jackson, and now I started self-medicating again to deal with the grief and the stress of working in Fort Worth. Was I really any better off? Had I lost touch with my family only to create my own other problems with drugs and alcohol?

These feelings hurt, and a lot of them involved shame. And any addict knows that shame can be deadly. Shame feeds addiction like nothing else.

And I was an addict, though I hadn't admitted this to anyone else, or even to myself. I began drinking more—a lot more—and smoking pot with people from work. I tried to be on the road as often as I could. It gave me an excuse to get away from home and take people out to dinner and drink and smoke and stay out late. All the while, the company saw I was working my butt off, going from city to city. But it was the alcohol and Adderall that made it possible. I was running away from responsibility and shame. I was throwing myself into my job. And I was self-medicating to make up the difference.

During this time, my wife was home with the kids. She knew me too well to believe any lies, so we simply didn't talk much about my lifestyle. She didn't ask the questions she knew I didn't know how to answer. I was grieving—she knew that—so a lot went unsaid during this time. But that was my fault. I knew she didn't approve of my constant traveling and we both knew it wasn't helping me grieve.

So the next year, we moved to Texas—to a little town west of Fort Worth called Aledo. While my mind was a mess, my job was working out, and I suspected (rightly) that it would be there for a while. The idea was to slow things down, be home more often, and begin to heal.

But that didn't really happen. I was in over my head.

I remember one night in San Francisco drinking a beer in my hotel room. It had been a long day, and I was, yet again, thousands of miles from home. I got a crazy idea at 9:30pm, called a cab, and went to a local bar. It was a karaoke bar in a pretty iffy part of town. I was here to sing.

It's not as crazy as it sounds. I'd done this once before, and I'd always liked to sing. My friends knew this about me, even if they liked to poke fun.

But this night in San Francisco, I was looking for a thrill. Singing in front of strangers was a dopamine hit, and I'd become addicted to that. The nerves, the release, the relief—the whole thing drew me in, and it was yet another excuse to go out and get drunk.

Over the next year or so, karaoke became part of my addiction. I liked it when people like what I did, and so I sang as much karaoke as I could. I followed particular DJs around. I had a routine. I'd do it with others, I'd do it alone. I'd do it in Texas, in California, in Florida—wherever I happened to be. I sought it out and did it almost every day after dinner, drink-in-hand and joint in my back pocket. I'd be out late, pass out back at the hotel, then do it all again the next day. My friends even got me a shirt once listing all the cities I'd sang in—there are more than 30 cities on that shirt. This became part of who I was to them, and I enjoyed the attention. It was fun.

But it was also a symptom of my deeper problems. Thoughts of my sister and my family lurked in the back of my mind, even on my busiest days. And I always had the pills and alcohol handy. But maybe, I thought, the more fun I could have and the more energy I could expend, the less I'd have to lay awake at night wondering about my family back at home and whether my wife was right—that this lifestyle wasn't going to work for very long.

> "Addiction, fueled by grief, becomes a monster. It turns you into a shadow of who you once were."

10

A TIME OF GRIEF

Grief is a beast.

It sneaks up on you, slowly wraps itself around your heart, and tightens its grip until every breath you take feels like a battle.

It's not something you can just shake off. It's sticky, like tar, and clings to every part of your being. It can turn your days into endless nights and your nights into a swirl of memories and regret. And it doesn't just visit now and then, either. It moves in, makes itself at home, and it changes you in ways you never thought possible.

And for someone battling addiction, grief is especially hard. When you're addicted to something, grief is a catalyst for all the worst things—a kind-of trigger that can send you spiraling into a darkness that seems inescapable.

My sister's death was a seismic event in my life. It shattered foundations I didn't even know I had.

My family had always been there. My relationship with them suffered after I got married, but they were fixtures in my life and had been for as long as I could remember. Even though I hadn't talked with them much, they were a part of my identity.

So when my sister died, part of me was thrown into a dark and confusing place. The pain, sometimes, was unbearable.

They say anger is one of the five stages of grief. I can attest to that. I was angry at God. Why do these bad things happen? Why do young people die? Why should we have to suffer from disease when life is already so hard?

These are age-old questions, I know. I think everyone has asked them at some point or other. But for me, in that time, they were as personal as they could possibly be. And I couldn't handle it.

Turning to alcohol and drugs seemed like the only way to numb the pain. I'd already been self-medicating, but "two-or-three drinks" became bottles. A toke "here and there" became a daily occurrence. I gave in to the grief and all that came with it. I refused to focus on my blessings. I fed my anger and frustration with all the worst things.

Any addict will tell you that, eventually, drug and alcohol abuse will distort your perception of reality. The high makes you believe that your pain is too great to bear, and that the only way to survive is to keep drowning yourself in whatever you can find. It's a vicious cycle. The more you drink, the more you numb the pain. But the more you numb the pain, the less you feel connected to the world around you, and the more isolated you become.

In my case, the grief over my sister's death turned my life into a blur of missed opportunities and broken relationships. I became a stranger to my own family. I felt like a ghost drifting through my own life. The alcohol and drugs created a wall that separated me from the people who loved me and from the hard realities I couldn't bear to face. I was there, but not really. My body was present, but my mind was lost in a fog of intoxication and denial.

I didn't look inside, because I was scared to see the bad parts of myself. I'd rather just look the other way. Do this for long enough, and you begin to feel unworthy of love, of happiness, of redemption. Hardly any piece of you really wants to get better. I began to believe that the only way to cope is to keep numbing the pain—to keep hiding from the truth.

Addiction, fueled by grief, becomes a monster. It takes control and demands more and more of your life, your time, your very essence. It feeds on your pain and grows stronger with every drink, every hit. And as it grows, it consumes everything in its path—your relationships, your job, your sense of self. It turns you into a shadow of the person you once were. You become a hollow shell of a human being, fixated only on the hit and the next moment of oblivion.

It twists your thoughts and amplifies your fears. It drags you deeper into the darkness. It makes you question everything you ever believed in and everything you ever loved. It makes you push away everyone who loves you and wants to help. It makes you feel alone, even in a room full of people, because you can only really think about one thing.

Within just a few months of my sister's death, I became completely trapped in this cycle. Alcohol and pot became my only coping mechanism. And somehow, I continued working at an incredible pace. Sometimes I'd be in three cities in one week, then back home on the weekend. It wasn't healthy and it wasn't right. My wife and kids deserved better. But living life at 60 mph was part of my plan to run away from my pain.

But a man can only run so long. And the pain was fast—always right behind me, no matter how far I ran.

> "We picked up the boys the next day…and we were committed to becoming a slightly bigger family—at least for the time being."

11

MY NEPHEWS

I don't remember much about the years after my sister's death.

I spent much of my time in a haze. I was still working like a dog. I'd often be gone all week long, meeting with clients from California to New York. When I was back home in Fort Worth, we pushed boundaries and never stopped. The pace was crazy, and I'd completely settled into my addictions. I was going through the motions, and I stepped outside for a smoke every chance I got. I'd hop in my truck, take a few tokes, smoke a cigarette, then pop a few mints and go back into work. I was stoned all the time.

But then something happened that began to change everything.

In 2015, I took my family back to Natchez to visit family. We'd lived in Texas for a few years by now, and we visited Natchez every so often. We had family and friends there and probably always will. This particular trip was to celebrate the Fourth of July.

As always, we drove straight through Louisiana and passed through Vidalia—right across the river from Natchez. My mom grew up there. Her dad was a musician—he was in the first band Jerry Lee Lewis ever played in before becoming a one-man band and playing all over the South. He even performed at the New Orleans Jazz and Heritage Festival.

He was known around there. A sort-of local legend, I guess. So Vidalia was a special place for my family. We even lived there for a while when I was a kid. My mom had a house in town which she eventually gave to my brother.

He wasn't doing well. Chesney had received a call from my sister's widow who lived down the street from the house my brother was living in. He said that Nate was bad off on drugs and the kids needed help. He said if someone didn't do something, Child Protective Services were going to take the kids.

I'd known that my brother had, like me, struggled with addiction. And like me, he'd had good times and bad times. I really didn't think much of it, or of him. I was pretty consumed with my own life and my own problems. And I was traveling like crazy.

But after my sister's death, there was no ignoring him. He was in bad shape. My wife told me before we left for Natchez that July that he and his fiancée were struggling. They had two boys and apparently they'd been seen outside at night—the younger one in a diaper—walking together down the street. They'd steal tomatoes from neighbors' gardens to eat. They were like feral kids.

I almost didn't believe this. But I walked into my brother's house in Vidalia that day, and I was shocked. It was a mess. My dad had moved in with my brother, and they were both high. The kids were running wild. Neither of them spoke well. They didn't know their colors, numbers, or even the difference between morning and evening. The younger one had a speech impediment and had almost created his own language.

That stuff hurts. I'd been prepared to see my brother in a rough spot. I had low expectations of him, and, subconsciously, I knew I wasn't going to be surprised by almost anything he might do. But to see his kids running around neglected and almost completely unkempt? That's hard. That stings.

We spoke for a few minutes. I gave him a hug, greeted my dad. Then I said we'd like to take the boys for a while. This was my wife's idea. I was a little skeptical, but seeing them in this state was more than enough "proof," for me, that we'd be wrong not to help them. I told my brother he needed help, and needed to get help, and that having the boys off his hands would mean more free time to do that.

He heard "free time" and agreed immediately.

We picked up the boys the next day. They each had a tiny, mismatched suitcase that reeked of cigarettes. They hopped in the car and we were committed to becoming a slightly bigger family—at least for the time being.

That time being turned into five years.

For three of those years, nobody checked on the boys. We didn't hear much from their parents. Their dad—my brother—asked for them back once, but agreed with me that he should be sober for at least a year before we talked about that. Sober never happened.

My wife and I didn't like that their parents checked out, but this allowed us to become their "adopted" parents. They called me dad and they called my wife mom. We loved them like our own. We put them in school, signed them up for sports. We got the younger one into speech therapy and everything about those boys and who they were got better. Their personalities came out and we became a new, bigger family. The boys were happy.

But all of this came at a cost that I wasn't willing, or even able, to acknowledge at the time.

The fact is, my wife bore this burden. People praised us both for the sacrifice we made, but it was my wife who insisted we take the boys in and who did most of the work. She was their mom every single day. Meanwhile, my life hadn't slowed down. I was traveling almost weekly and and I was still hiding (with minimal success) my drug and alcohol addiction.

By 2017, that stress hit a breaking point. My wife decided we needed to move back to Natchez. We had more family and friends there, and she needed more support raising four kids. I agreed, but so long as my job and my addiction consumed so much of my energy, there was no real possibility that this was going to "work."

On September 2, 2018, I packed my things and moved out.

> "The fog of addiction was lifting, and I was rediscovering parts of myself I thought were lost forever."

12

MY EXPERIENCE IN REHAB

I didn't just up and leave that day. The decision to move out was the culmination of months of tension, lies, and broken promises. My wife had been patient, perhaps too patient, with my addiction for years. She had watched me spiral, seen the toll it was taking on our family, and finally reached her breaking point.

A few months before I left, she confronted me with an ultimatum. Her eyes were filled with a mixture of love, disappointment, and determination as she said, "I can't keep living like this. You need to get drug-tested every week. If you don't, or if you fail even once, we're done." Her voice cracked slightly, betraying the pain behind her words. I nodded, not fully grasping the gravity of the situation, still convinced I could manage both my addiction and my family life.

For a while, I managed to pass these tests using a fake sample. It was a dance of deception—I'd carefully prepare the sample, hide it on my person, and swap it out during the test. Each time I successfully fooled the test, I felt a twisted sense of victory. But deep down, I knew I was only digging myself deeper into a hole of lies and betrayal.

The charade couldn't last forever. One fateful day, as I was rushing out to go help my nephew look at his truck , I carelessly left my one-hitter in the door of my truck. It was a rookie mistake, born from the complacency that comes with thinking you've outsmarted everyone. My wife, probably suspecting something was amiss, decided to check my vehicle that day.

I remember the moment vividly. I got back home to find her standing in the living room, arms crossed, my one-hitter clutched in her hand. The look on her face—a mixture of hurt, anger, and resigned disappointment—is something I'll never forget. In that instant, I knew the game was up. All my lies, all my deceptions, came crashing down around me. The carefully constructed facade I had built to protect my addiction crumbled, leaving me exposed and vulnerable.

I moved out the next day.

At first, I felt like a free man. I spent the next 10 days in my corporate apartment, indulging in a haze of marijuana and alcohol, doing whatever I wanted without restraint. It was a lonely existence, but not the kind of loneliness I was accustomed to. Years of traveling for work had hardened me to being alone in hotels and corporate apartments, but this isolation was different—it was saturated with anger, regret, and a profound sense of loss.

The freedom I thought I'd gain by leaving my family quickly revealed itself as an illusion. Instead of feeling liberated, I found myself trapped in a cycle of self-destructive behavior. I'd wake up each morning, promising myself that today would be different, only to fall back into the same patterns by nightfall. The weight of what I'd done—shattering my wife's heart, abandoning my children—bore down on me with crushing force.

I constantly wrestled with the question, "Why can't you get better?" It echoed in my mind during every waking moment, a relentless reminder of my failures. This wasn't the life I wanted, but I felt utterly powerless to change it. The addiction had its claws so deep in me that the very thought of permanent sobriety seemed impossible. I would quit for a while, making earnest promises to myself and others that I would stay clean, only to succumb to the siren call of drugs and alcohol when the cravings became too intense or life too overwhelming.

As the days passed, I prepared for a conference in Austin. I knew this would be another test of my already fragile willpower. Conferences had always been a minefield for me—long days of networking seamlessly blending into nights of heavy drinking and partying. This conference proved no different. We hit the bars with a vengeance, played pool until the early hours, and belted out off-key karaoke tunes. I tried to lose myself in the revelry, to recapture some semblance of the carefree person I used to be, but it was futile.

Beneath the forced smiles and laughter, thoughts of my broken family and uncertain future nagged at me incessantly. The faces of my wife and children would flash before my eyes, their disappointment and hurt palpable even in my imagination. Each time I raised a glass to my lips or inhaled the acrid smoke of a joint, I felt a stab of guilt, knowing I was betraying not just them, but also myself and the promises I'd made. I had become the very thing I hated about my dad.

It was in the quiet moments, when the noise of the day faded and I was left alone with my thoughts, that the true weight of my situation hit me. Lying in my bed, staring at the ceiling, the enormity of what I'd lost—and what I stood to lose if I didn't change—would wash over me. The guilt, the shame, the fear of an uncertain future—it all came crashing down, threatening to crush me beneath its weight. Most nights, it did.

They say one of the most dangerous things for a man is to be left alone with his thoughts, and I felt the truth of that statement deep in my bones. In those silent hours, my mind became a battlefield, with regret, self-loathing, and the desperate desire to change waging war against the insidious pull of addiction. I'd lie awake, bargaining with myself, with God, with anyone who would listen, promising that tomorrow would be different. But as the sun rose and a new day began, I found myself reaching for the bottle or the joint once more, trapped in a cycle I couldn't seem to break.

It was during one of these long, sleepless nights that I realized something had to give. I couldn't continue living this half-life, caught between the person I wanted to be and the addict I'd become. The path ahead was unclear and terrifying, but I knew that if I didn't take the first step towards change, I risked losing everything I held dear. Both of my daughters had written me letters begging me to get better, and asking why I would choose to abandon them for drugs. With trembling hands and a racing heart, I made a decision that would alter the course of my life forever—I decided to seek help.

By the end of the week, I decided enough was enough. On September 12th, 2018, I smoked and drank for the last time. The detox that followed was brutal. For two and a half weeks, I endured night sweats, irritability, no appetite, and severe stomach cramps. People often say marijuana isn't addictive, but detoxing from the amount I used felt like coming off heroin. It was a physical and mental ordeal, and I struggled with breaking the daily habits that had defined my life. Most of all, I didn't know who I was without the drugs. I had to rediscover my identity, and that was terrifying.

Living with an addict is tough for any family, and sobriety doesn't automatically make things easier. When you get clean, you become a different person—someone your family might not recognize. This can lead to frustration and anger on both sides. Despite these challenges, Chesney and I decided that moving back to Natchez wasn't working. The girls hated it there, and we agreed to return to Texas.

When we moved back, Chesney made it clear I had to prove my commitment to sobriety. She set strict boundaries and told me I needed to get help. This wasn't just a suggestion. It was an ultimatum. I knew that if I wanted to salvage my marriage and be there for my children, I had to take this seriously.

My Experience in Rehab

After researching various options, I checked into an outpatient rehab program in Fort Worth. The program was intensive, requiring me to attend sessions for four hours a day, five days a week. It was a significant time commitment, but I was determined to make it work. Looking back, I can confidently say that this was the best decision I ever made.

Rehab wasn't just about quitting substances. It was about unpacking my past and understanding the roots of my addiction. The program took a holistic approach, addressing not only the physical aspects of addiction but also the psychological and emotional components. We had group therapy sessions where we shared our experiences and struggles, individual counseling to dive deeper into personal issues, and educational seminars about the science of addiction and recovery.

The therapy sessions were particularly challenging but incredibly rewarding. They helped me confront painful memories that I had been avoiding for years—my dad's leaving when I was young, my sister's battle with cancer, and the trauma that came with those experiences. For the first time, I was able to process these events in a healthy way, guided by trained professionals and supported by peers who understood what I was going through.

One of the most profound realizations I had during rehab was how much my past experiences had shaped my behavior and choices. I began to see patterns in my life that I had never noticed before. The coping mechanisms I had developed—using substances to numb pain or escape reality—suddenly made sense in the context of my history. This understanding didn't excuse my actions, but it gave me a starting point for change.

The program also taught me practical skills for maintaining sobriety. We learned about trigger management, stress reduction techniques, and how to build a support network. I discovered the importance of self-care and how to deal with cravings and urges in a healthy way. These tools proved invaluable in the months and years that followed.

Throughout the rehab process, Chesney remained supportive but firm. She attended family therapy sessions with me, which helped us rebuild trust and improve our communication. It wasn't easy for either of us, but I could see that she was committed to our relationship if I was willing to do the work.

As I progressed through the program, I began to feel a sense of hope that I hadn't experienced in years. The fog of addiction was lifting, and I was rediscovering parts of myself that I thought were lost forever. It was a long and challenging journey, but with each passing day, I felt stronger and more capable of facing life without the crutch of substances.

Before rehab, I had seen a therapist who justified my addiction, telling me my wife was the problem. Many of our mutual friends told me Chesney just wanted to control me and I didn't have a problem. One of them would even give me Adderall even though they knew I had a problem with it. This mindset is dangerous. It perpetuates the cycle of addiction. In rehab, I sat with other addicts, sharing stories and realizing I was better off than many others. I had people who genuinely loved me, even if I couldn't live with them yet. Therapy taught me that sobriety requires patience, a trait I wasn't comfortable with. My identity had been tied to my addiction for so long that I didn't know how to be sober. I struggled with breaking daily habits—getting in my truck and not reaching for my one-hitter was a constant battle. But the thought of never getting high or drunk again was terrifying. I couldn't imagine a different future.

It was around this time that we started attending Life Church with Pastor Craig Groeschel. His sermon series, "Mastermind: Change Your Thinking, Change Your Life," was transformative. He preached that our lives move in the direction of our strongest thoughts. This concept resonated deeply with me, as I had spent years allowing negative thoughts to dominate my mind and drive my actions. Pastor Groeschel's words offered a glimmer of hope—a way to rewire my brain and, potentially, my life.

Inspired by his teachings, I decided to practice this mindset shift, consciously reframing negative thoughts into positive ones. It wasn't easy at first. Years of addiction had ingrained patterns of self-doubt, fear, and pessimism. Every morning, I'd wake up and immediately be bombarded by anxious thoughts about the day ahead. But instead of succumbing to them, I'd pause and deliberately reframe each thought. "I can't handle this" became "I have the strength to face today's challenges." "I'll never stay sober" transformed into "Every day, I'm growing stronger in my recovery."

This practice was a daily battle, requiring constant vigilance and effort. There were moments when I felt ridiculous, forcing myself to think positively when everything seemed bleak. But I persisted, reminding myself of Pastor Groeschel's words and the potential for change they held. Gradually, I began to notice shifts in my outlook and behavior. The constant cloud of negativity that had followed me for years started to dissipate, replaced by a cautious optimism.

As weeks turned into months, this new way of thinking began to reshape my entire outlook on life. I found myself approaching challenges with a sense

My Experience in Rehab

of capability rather than dread. Relationships that had been strained by my addiction started to heal as I brought a more positive energy to our interactions. Even my work performance improved as I focused on possibilities rather than limitations.

For the next 18 to 24 months, I diligently practiced this new way of thinking. It became a cornerstone of my recovery, a daily exercise as crucial as attending meetings or avoiding triggers. The transformation was gradual but profound. One day, I realized I hadn't had a truly negative thought in a long time. The anger that had fueled my addiction for so long had dissipated, replaced by a sense of peace and purpose I had never known before.

This shift wasn't just internal. Those around me began to notice the change. Colleagues commented on my improved mood and productivity. Friends remarked on how much easier I was to be around. But most importantly, my family saw the difference. Chesney, who had stood by me through the darkest times, watched with a mixture of joy and relief as I became the person she had always believed I could be.

This practice of positive thinking did more than just keep me sober—it brought an immense joy and sense of fulfillment into my life that I had never experienced before. I found myself genuinely excited about the future, eager to see what each new day would bring. The world, which had once seemed like a hostile place full of temptations and pitfalls, now appeared full of opportunities and beauty.

Chesney's unwavering belief in me throughout this journey was a constant source of strength. She had always insisted that the person I became in my addiction wasn't the real me. She saw potential in me that I couldn't see in myself, envisioning a life for us that seemed impossible during the depths of my struggle. For years, she couldn't understand why I didn't see what she saw, why I couldn't break free from the cycle of addiction and negativity.

Now, as I embraced this new mindset and way of living, I was finally becoming the person Chesney had always believed I could be. It was as if a veil had been lifted, allowing me to see myself and the world around me with new clarity. The transformation wasn't just about sobriety—it was about rediscovering my true self, the person who had been buried beneath years of addiction and negative thinking.

This journey of mental change taught me the true power of our thoughts. It showed me that change, no matter how difficult it might seem, is always possible. By consciously directing our thoughts, we can reshape our reality and create the life we truly desire. For me, this meant not just achieving

My Experience in Rehab

sobriety, but finding a deep sense of purpose, joy, and connection that I had never thought possible.

And when it comes to my work, the timing couldn't have been better. In January 2019, our company was sold to a larger, publicly traded company. I was deeply involved in the process from beginning to end, providing data and analysis to both parties to the deal. Looking back, I'm lucky I got sober before this happened. The buyer's strict policies on drugs and alcohol could have cost me everything. Maybe this timing was God at work.

The next six years of my life were a transformative journey of sobriety and leadership development. While my history had always been marked by hard work, true leadership only emerged as I embraced sobriety. Looking back, I can see that even during periods where I managed to be a decent leader, my potential was overshadowed by my addiction. Now, free from the chains of substance abuse, I had the opportunity to become the leader I had always aspired to be, firmly grounded in reality and sobriety.

The transformation was far from easy. It required me to confront my demons head-on and rebuild my life from the ground up. Each day presented its own set of challenges as I struggled to maintain my new habits and mindset. I made a conscious decision to wake up every morning with a determined attitude of gratitude. This practice became my anchor, reminding me of the good things in my life—my loving family, my improving health, and my financial stability. In a world often filled with chaos and struggle, I recognized that I had much to be thankful for.

I began to see my journey through a new lens. Instead of viewing sobriety as a restriction, I saw it as an opportunity for growth and self-discovery. This shift in perspective allowed me to approach challenges with a newfound sense of resilience and optimism. I started to notice small victories that I might have overlooked before—a productive day at work, a meaningful conversation with my children, or a moment of peace and clarity. These seemingly minor achievements began to accumulate, reinforcing my commitment to this new way of life.

As I progressed in my recovery, I started to recognize the profound impact my addiction had on my leadership abilities. In the past, my decision-making was often clouded by substance abuse, leading to inconsistent performance and strained relationships with colleagues and employees. Now, with a clear mind and renewed focus, I could approach my professional responsibilities with integrity and dedication. I found myself more present in meetings, more attentive to the needs of my team, and more capable of strategic long-term planning.

Motivational speakers often extol the power of positive thinking, but I quickly learned that putting this into practice is far more challenging than it sounds. It's all too easy to fall back into old patterns of negative self-talk and pessimistic outlooks. Recognizing this, I made a conscious effort to reframe my thoughts constantly. I developed a habit of catching negative thoughts before they could take root, challenging them, and replacing them with more constructive alternatives. This wasn't just about forcing myself to "think happy thoughts"—it was about cultivating a realistic yet optimistic mindset that could weather life's inevitable ups and downs.

Over time, this practice of positive reframing became second nature. I found myself naturally gravitating towards more constructive thought patterns. The change wasn't just internal—it manifested in tangible ways in my daily life. I discovered joy and happiness in places I never thought possible. Simple pleasures, like a quiet morning coffee or a walk in nature, took on new significance. Most importantly, my connection with my family deepened significantly. I became more present in their lives, truly listening and engaging rather than just going through the motions.

Throughout this journey, Chesney's relentless support was my bedrock. She had always seen the potential in me, even when I couldn't see it myself. Her belief in the man I could become never faltered, even during my darkest moments. Looking back, I'm filled with profound gratitude for her patience, love, and determination. She saw the life we could have together and never gave up on that vision, even when I had lost sight of it myself.

As I reflect on the past six years, I can say without hesitation that they have been the happiest and most fulfilling of my life. This period has been characterized by a deep sense of joy, love, and purpose that I never thought possible during my years of addiction. My journey through sobriety has taught me invaluable lessons about resilience, patience, and the transformative power of positive thinking.

These lessons extend far beyond my personal life—they've fundamentally changed how I approach leadership and business. I've learned that true leadership isn't about having all the answers or never making mistakes. Instead, it's about fostering an environment of trust, open communication, and continuous growth. My experiences have given me a unique perspective on human struggle and resilience, allowing me to lead with greater empathy and understanding.

As I continue on this path, I'm committed to using my experiences to help others. Whether it's mentoring employees who may be struggling with their own challenges or sharing my story with those battling addiction, I believe that my journey can serve as a beacon of hope. It's a testament to the fact that no matter how dire circumstances may seem, change is always possible with determination, support, and a willingness to face one's demons head-on.

The road ahead is not without its challenges, but I face them with a sense of optimism and purpose that would have been unimaginable just a few years ago. My journey of sobriety and leadership development continues to unfold, each day bringing new opportunities for growth, connection, and positive impact. As I look to the future, I'm filled with excitement for what lies ahead, grateful for how far I've come, and committed to continuing this journey of self-improvement and service to others.

"Without accountability, real growth is impossible—personally, professionally, spiritually."

13

I FIND THE OTHER SIDE

It's been more than six years since I committed to sobriety, and it's time to unpack the journey. My story of addiction, trauma, and the battles I fought during my darkest moments shaped who I am today. It wasn't just about getting clean—it was about learning to lead with empathy, clarity, and accountability. Through sobriety, I became a better leader, a better listener, and someone who could genuinely connect with the people around me on a deeper level.

At the height of my addiction, my thinking was clouded. My mind was scattered, jumping from one thought to another, weighed down by negativity and doubt. I was just trying to survive, let alone thrive as a leader. But as I navigated sobriety, I realized how much those struggles were teaching me, even then. They were setting the stage for me to understand what real leadership looks like. Now, I oversee more than 400 employees, but back when I was in the early stages of my recovery, it wasn't easy.

In the beginning, I had to retrain my mind—eliminating negative thoughts and refocusing on achievable goals. Daily, weekly, and monthly milestones became my markers for success, not just in my personal life but in how I managed my organizations. It wasn't enough to be just the boss. I needed to be someone my employees could trust, someone who listened to their concerns, someone who genuinely cared.

Before sobriety, I thought I was connecting with my team, but I was wrong. I was being a people pleaser, focused only on a small fraction of my team while ignoring the bigger picture. I learned to sit with my employees, work through their issues, and, more importantly, show them I cared. When someone came to me asking for a raise or more hours because they needed to support their family, I could truly empathize with them. Addiction taught me about loneliness, about trying to fill a void that nothing seems to satisfy. That feeling, that hunger for connection, allowed me to relate to others on a much deeper level.

One of the most significant things I've learned in both sobriety and leadership is accountability—not just to others but to myself. Before I could become a better leader, I had to face the truth about who I was and what I had done. Therapy helped me see that

I Find the Other Side

I wasn't being accountable to myself. I was relying on others for happiness, which is a dead end. I had to learn how to be self-reliant, to look in the mirror every day with raw truth and grace, asking myself, "What can I do better?"

It's not easy. When someone—whether it's an employee or my spouse—comes to me with a problem or calls me out for something I've done, it's tempting to get defensive. But I've learned to pause, put myself in their shoes, and ask, "Would I be okay with being treated this way?" More often than not, the answer is no, and that's when I know I need to apologize, take responsibility, and move forward.

The longer I've stayed sober, the more I've realized how essential accountability is in every aspect of life. When I look around, I see so many people, especially leaders, struggling with it. They don't want to hold themselves accountable. They don't want to look in the mirror and make real, lasting changes.

But without accountability, real growth is impossible.

That's why I invite constructive criticism. I regularly ask my team to challenge me, to help me see where I can improve. In 2021, when I took over my company after we sold it, I made it a point to shift our focus. Before, our CEO had been so fixated on big clients—banks, lending institutions, and the like—that we neglected the smaller, hardworking customers who provided us with our bread and butter: repossession agencies. These were gritty, blue-collar people who were vital to our success, but their voices had been ignored. I knew that had to change.

We began listening to them, addressing their concerns, and treating them with the respect they deserved. It wasn't easy—there was a lot of cleanup to do—but I made it a personal goal to give every customer, big or small, the same attention. It was a matter of putting people before profit, something I learned was vital not only in business but in life. In recovery, I had to face my demons and admit I had a problem. I had to do the same in business, owning up to the flaws in our company and working to fix them.

Looking back, I see how addiction forced me to learn one of the most valuable lessons in leadership: vulnerability. Standing in a circle, admitting to a group of strangers that I had a problem, was one of the hardest things I've ever done. But that accountability—owning my past, my pain, and my mistakes—became the foundation of my leadership style. It taught me to listen, to care, and to respond with empathy.

In those moments of vulnerability, I saw how closely connected accountability in recovery is to accountability in business. Both require looking in the mirror, facing hard truths, and committing to change. It's not just about running a company but about leading with compassion, giving people the space to voice their concerns, and taking responsibility for the impact you have on others.

There's a lot of talk about legacy. For some, it's about leaving behind wealth or success. But for me, my legacy is about the people I've impacted. The employees I've mentored, the customers I've helped, and the lives I've touched. Sobriety has shown me that true success isn't measured by profits or accolades—it's measured by the relationships you build and the lives you change.

Sobriety gave me back my life, but it also gave me the tools to be the leader I never thought I could be. It taught me that vulnerability isn't weakness. Vulnerability is strength. It taught me that people are looking for leaders who are real, who can admit their mistakes and work to fix them. That's the legacy I want to leave behind—not just as a businessman, but as someone who made a difference in the lives of others.

> "Your job as a leader is to keep people aligned with the bigger picture—not to obsess over every detail of how it's executed."

14

MOVING FORWARD

These days, people often ask me how I manage it all. "How do you do it?" they say, their eyes wide with a mix of curiosity and disbelief. And I understand their reaction because, on the surface, my life might seem overwhelming, even impossible to some. I run three separate companies, each with its own unique challenges and demands. Together, these businesses require me to oversee 420 people—that's 420 individuals with their own needs, goals, and potential issues that might need my attention at any given moment.

But that's just the professional side of things. I recently earned a Master's Degree at SMU, which involves countless hours of study, research, and writing papers. It's a commitment I've made to further my education and broaden my horizons, even as I navigate the complex world of business leadership. And let's not forget the most important part of my life: my family. Despite all these responsibilities,

I make it a priority to be present for my loved ones, to be an active part of their lives, not just a distant figure always buried in work.

When people hear all this, they're often left wondering how I keep up. How do I juggle all these roles and responsibilities without falling apart at the seams? They're looking for some secret formula, some magic trick that allows me to fit 30 hours of activity into a 24-hour day. But the truth is, there's no sleight of hand involved. It's not about having superhuman abilities or sacrificing sleep (though I'll admit, there are nights when sleep does take a backseat).

The reality is, I never feel like I have a great answer to their questions. At least, not one that satisfies their curiosity in the way they expect. They're often looking for a step-by-step guide, a blueprint for success that they can follow. But life, especially a life filled with as many moving parts as mine, doesn't work that way. There's no one-size-fits-all solution, no universal roadmap to follow.

So, how do I do it? How do I keep all these plates spinning without everything crashing down around me? It's not magic, and it's certainly not a secret formula that I'm keeping to myself. When it all boils down, my answer is simple, perhaps deceptively so: gratitude. This single word, this powerful concept, is at the core of everything I do, every decision I make, and every challenge I face.

Gratitude isn't just a feel-good buzzword for me. It's a fundamental shift in perspective that colors how I see the world and my place in it. It's about waking up each morning and, instead of feeling overwhelmed by the day ahead, feeling profoundly thankful for the opportunities that await me. It's about seeing each challenge not as a burden, but as a chance to grow, to learn, to become better than I was yesterday.

This attitude of gratitude doesn't make the work any easier, but it does make it more meaningful. It doesn't reduce the number of hours in my day, but it does help me make the most of each one. When you're grateful for what you have and the opportunities before you, you approach tasks with a different energy. You're not just going through the motions. When you're truly grateful, you're engaged, you're present, you're purposeful.

So while it might not be the answer people are expecting, gratitude is truly the foundation that allows me to manage it all. It's what gets me out of bed in the morning, ready to face whatever challenges the day might bring. It's what keeps me going when the hours grow long and the tasks seem endless. And most importantly, it's what reminds me, every single day, how fortunate I am to have this life, with all its complexities and demands. Because at the end of the day, I wouldn't have it any other way.

Every day, I wake up with an overwhelming sense of gratitude. I don't take for granted the opportunities I've been given or the people around me who make it all possible. This attitude of gratitude is the foundation for everything I do. But people don't always get how that ties into managing multiple companies, addressing budgets, dealing with complaints, and keeping up with endless responsibilities.

We've all read leadership books and admired successful CEOs, wondering how they manage to keep their ships afloat. We've looked up to these people as if they have some secret sauce that makes everything easier. But for me, the secret is simple—it's not about focusing on the mechanics. It's about focusing on the people around you. We tend to get caught up in the details. We want to know how everything gets done, step by step, and we let that overwhelm us. But that's not where our focus should be, especially as leaders. If you trust the people around you, the ones you've hired and invested in, the ones you've built up, you can let go of micromanaging the mechanics and start seeing the bigger picture. Your job as a leader is to keep people aligned with that bigger picture, not to obsess over every detail of how it's executed.

I've been fortunate to have been surrounded by great leaders in my time—people I could observe and learn from. One of the most important lessons I've picked up is that leadership is about trust—trusting your team to carry out their roles and responsibilities and trusting yourself to guide them toward success. If you've done your due diligence in hiring the right people, then you should be able to let go. Focus on the vision the direction, and let your team handle the details. And if something goes wrong, yes, it's your responsibility to step in and help find a solution, but trust that your people are capable of figuring it out.

Lead with gratitude. Empower others. The rest will take care of itself.

A little over a year ago, I experienced a situation that reinforced the importance of this mindset. We were at a conference, and like many industry events, it involved a lot of socializing—and, unfortunately, a lot of drinking. I've been sober for years, but not everyone at these events practices moderation. Some treat it like it's spring break all over again. The atmosphere can be challenging for those of us in recovery, but it's also an opportunity to practice resilience and lead by example.

I was outside with some friends and business partners, sitting around a fire pit, enjoying the cool evening air and engaging in lively conversation. The night was going well, filled with laughter and meaningful discussions about our industry's future. It was during one of these moments of camaraderie that a man approached our group. He was clearly inebriated, swaying slightly as he walked, his eyes unfocused. Though I didn't know him personally, I recognized him as a customer from one of our smaller agencies.

He sat down heavily next to me, extending his hand for a shake. As I grasped it, I could feel the tension in his grip. He muttered something under his breath, too low for me to catch at first. I didn't pay much attention to it, chalking it up to the effects of alcohol. But as the night wore on, I could sense his agitation growing. His body language became more aggressive, his voice rising with each passing minute.

Soon, he started accusing me of running my business unfairly, claiming I was showing favoritism to another agency. His words were slurred, but the anger behind them was palpable. The alcohol was only amplifying his emotions, turning what might have been a minor grievance into a full-blown confrontation. Other members of our group began to shift uncomfortably, sensing the growing tension.

Moving Forward

In that moment, I knew I had a choice to make. I could have matched his aggression, defended myself vehemently against his accusations. Part of me wanted to—after all, I've worked hard to build my business ethically and fairly. The old me, the one before sobriety, might have escalated the situation. We could have been in a fistfight within minutes, causing a scene and potentially damaging both our reputations.

But something inside me, a voice honed by years of recovery and self-reflection, told me that wasn't the answer. I took a deep breath, centering myself. I thought about the gratitude I felt for my sobriety, for the second chance I'd been given in life. I remembered all the times I'd been in his shoes, angry and drunk, lashing out at the world.

Instead of reacting with anger, I stayed calm. I looked him in the eye and said, "I hear that you're upset, and your feelings are valid. But right now isn't the best time to have this conversation. Why don't we discuss this in the morning when we're both clear-headed? I promise to listen to your concerns and address them fairly."

My response seemed to catch him off guard. He stared at me for a moment, his anger momentarily forgotten. Then, without another word, he stood up and stumbled away. The tension in our group dissipated, and conversation slowly resumed. But I couldn't shake the encounter from my mind. I knew there was more to his outburst than just alcohol and business disagreements.

The next morning, as I was having breakfast in the hotel restaurant, his business manager approached my table. The man's face was a mixture of embarrassment and concern. He apologized profusely for his bosses' behavior the night before, explaining that it was completely out of character. He asked if we could talk, to clear the air and address any issues. I agreed, seeing an opportunity not just to resolve a business matter, but potentially to help someone in need.

When we finally sat down later that day, the man—let's call him Jim—was a different person from the angry, intoxicated individual I'd encountered the night before. His face was pale, eyes bloodshot, likely nursing a severe hangover. But more than that, he looked defeated. He apologized immediately, clearly embarrassed by his actions.

As we talked, I could see that Jim was deeply troubled. The anger from the previous night had given way to vulnerability. He opened up about the immense stress he was under, both professionally and personally. His business was struggling, barely staying afloat in an increasingly competitive market.

At home, his marriage was on the rocks, strained by his long hours and increasing reliance on alcohol to cope.

Jim confessed that he felt like he was failing at work, failing his family, and turning to alcohol more and more to numb the pain and anxiety. His outburst at me, he explained, wasn't really about business practices or favoritism. It was the culmination of months of stress, fear, and self-doubt, all amplified by alcohol.

As I listened to Jim's story, I felt a profound sense of empathy. I saw in him a reflection of my past self—a man struggling with the weight of his responsibilities, using alcohol as a crutch, and lashing out at others as a way to externalize his inner turmoil. In that moment, I knew that this conversation had the potential to be about much more than just clearing the air over a drunken misunderstanding. It could be a turning point in Jim's life, just as I had experienced my own turning point years ago.

I told Jim my story. I shared my journey with addiction and how it nearly destroyed my life, my marriage, and my career. I opened up about the darkest moments, the times when I felt utterly lost and hopeless. I described the toll it took on my relationships, how I pushed away the people who cared about me most. I recounted the sleepless nights, the constant anxiety, and the overwhelming shame that accompanied my addiction.

As I spoke, I could see the shock in Jim's eyes. He couldn't believe that someone like me, someone he viewed as successful and put-together, had gone through the same struggles he was facing. I saw a glimmer of recognition in his expression, a silent acknowledgment of our shared experience. And that's when I realized something important: vulnerability is not a weakness—it's a strength. It's the courage to be seen, truly seen, with all our flaws and imperfections.

Sharing my story with Jim wasn't about telling him how to live his life. It wasn't about preaching or lecturing. It was about showing him that change is possible, that the darkness he was experiencing wasn't permanent. I wanted him to understand that his current struggles didn't define him, just as mine hadn't defined me. I shared the steps I took to reclaim my life, the support systems I leaned on, and the daily practices that helped me maintain my sobriety.

In that moment, I didn't care about the business. I didn't care about the accusations he'd made the night before. What mattered to me was helping him get his life back on track. I saw in Jim a reflection of my past self, and I knew that with the right support and guidance, he could turn his life around too.

Over the next several months, I checked in on Jim regularly, offering support and encouragement. We had long conversations about addiction, recovery, and the challenges of balancing personal struggles with professional responsibilities. I connected him with resources in his area, including support groups and therapists specializing in addiction. I even offered to speak with his wife, to help her understand what Jim was going through and how she could support him in his journey to recovery.

It wasn't always easy. There were setbacks and moments of doubt. But Jim was committed to change, and I was committed to supporting him. Slowly but surely, we started to see progress. Jim began attending AA meetings regularly. He started therapy to address the underlying issues that had led to his addiction. He even took a short leave from work to focus on his recovery, a decision I fully supported and encouraged.

Today, Jim is sober. His marriage, once on the brink of collapse, is stronger than ever. His wife has become his biggest supporter, attending Al-Anon meetings to better understand addiction and how to support Jim in his recovery. His business, which had been struggling under the weight of his addiction, is now thriving. Jim's newfound clarity and focus have breathed new life into his work, and his team has rallied around him, inspired by his honesty and determination.

Of course, Jim still has his ups and downs. Recovery is a lifelong journey, not a destination. But his life has changed for the better in ways he never thought possible. He's rediscovered his passion for his work, rebuilt trust with his family, and found a new sense of purpose in helping others who are struggling with addiction.

This experience with Jim reaffirmed my belief that gratitude and vulnerability are essential components of leadership. It's not about projecting an image of perfection or pretending to have all the answers. It's about being real, being open, and being willing to help others, even when it means exposing our own wounds and imperfections.

When you approach every day with gratitude, you see challenges as opportunities for growth. You recognize that even the darkest moments can lead to profound transformations. And when you're vulnerable enough to share your struggles, you give others permission to do the same. You create a space where honesty and authenticity can flourish, where people feel safe to confront their own challenges and seek help.

In the end, my experience with Jim taught me that true leadership isn't about titles or achievements. It's about the impact we have on others' lives. It's about using our own experiences, even the painful ones, to light the way for others who are still finding their path. And it's about recognizing that in helping others, we often find deeper meaning and purpose in our own lives.

As leaders, we have a responsibility to be examples for those around us—not just through our successes, but through our struggles as well. I've come to realize that my purpose in life is not just to run successful businesses, but to help as many people as I can by sharing my story. Whether it's through my own experiences with addiction or through helping others navigate their own struggles, I believe that by leading with gratitude and vulnerability, we can make a real difference.

At the end of the day, success isn't about the numbers on a balance sheet. It's about the people we impact, the lives we touch, and the legacy we leave behind. And for me, that legacy is about showing others that no matter how dark things may seem, there's always a way forward. With gratitude, with vulnerability, and with a little help along the way, we can all find the strength to keep moving forward.

IN MEMORY OF ROBERT MORRIS

In loving memory of Robert Morris—a mentor, a teacher, and a friend. Your belief in me came at a time when I needed it most. You taught me that work is about more than profit—it's about people, integrity, and purpose. Your example shaped the man, the leader, and the father I became. Thank you for seeing potential in a young kid who didn't yet see it in himself. Your impact will echo through my life and the lives of everyone you inspired. You are deeply missed.

www.ingramcontent.com/pod-product-compliance
Lightning Source LLC
Chambersburg PA
CBHW032231080426
42735CB00008B/798